THE EMPOWERING UNIQUENESS

TOWARDS SOCIAL, YOUTH AND NATURE REFORMATION

KETAN. V. FIRKE

ISBN 979-888530086-5

"The Empowering Uniqueness - Towards Social, Youth and Nature Reformation" book is dedicated to my motherland and especially to the youths of our nation by thoughts and not by age. The inclination towards these parameters is to treat every human being with equal respect and dignity along with being true humanitarian.

Contents

Contents

Swami Vivekananda Quoted Some Important Points On Youth

- Go, all of you, wherever there is an outbreak of plague or famine, or wherever the people are in distress, and mitigate their sufferings...Preach This ideal from door to door, and you will yourselves be benefit by it at the same time that you are doing good to your country. On you lie the future hopes of our country.

- Freedom can never be reached by the weak. Throw away all weakness. Tell your body that it is strong, tell your mind that it is strong, and have unbounded faith and hope in yourself.

- "My hope of the future lies in the youths of character, intelligent, renouncing all for the service of others, and obedient – good to themselves and the country at large"

- "Act on the educated young men, bring them together, and organize them. Great things can be done by great sacrifices only. No selfishness, no name, No fame, yours or mine, nor my Master's even! Work, work the idea, the Plan, my boys, my brave, noble, good souls - to the wheel, to the wheel put your shoulders!"

- "Please everybody without becoming a hypocrite and without being a Coward. Hold on to your own ideas with strength and purity, and whatever Obstructions may now be in your way, the world is bound to listen to you in the long run. . . ."

- "Talk to yourself once in a day...Otherwise, you may miss meeting an EXCELLENT person in this World"

- "It is very easy to point out the defects of institutions, all being more or less Imperfect, but he is the real benefactor of humanity who helps the Individual to overcome his imperfections under whatever institutions he May live."

- Onward! Upon ages of struggle, a character is built. Be not discouraged. One Word of truth can never be lost; for ages, it may be hidden under rubbish, but it will show itself sooner or later. Truth is indestructible, virtue is Indestructible, and purity is indestructible.

- "Neither money pays, nor name pays, nor fame, nor learning; it is CHARACTER that cleaves through adamantine walls of difference."
- I stand for truth. The truth will never ally itself with falsehood. Even if all the world should be against me, Truth must prevail in the end.
- "Learn everything that is good from others, but bring it in, and in your own way absorb it; do not become others. Do not be dragged away out of this Indian life; do not for a moment think that it would be better for India if all the Indians dressed, ate, and behaved like another race."
- "We have to bear in mind that we are all debtors to the world & the world does not owe us anything. It is a great privilege for all of us to be allowed to do anything for the world. In helping the world we really help ourselves."
- Let your preparations be wise, correct and of such kind that will lead to your true welfare, supreme good and lasting satisfaction and happiness. This must engage your active, enthusiastic attention throughout the period of your youth life.
- Supreme value of youth period is incalculable and indescribable. Youth life is the most precious life. Youth is the best time. The way in which you utilize this period will decide the nature of coming years that lie ahead of you.
- "The infinite future is before you, and you must always remember that each word, thought, and deed, lays up a store for you and that as the bad thoughts and bad works are ready to spring upon you like tigers, so also there is the inspiring hope that the good thoughts and good deeds are ready with the power of a hundred thousand angels to defend you always and forever."

- "The earth is enjoyed by heroes—this is the unfailing truth. Be a hero.
  Always say, "I have no fear."
- My faith is in the younger generation, the modern generation, out of them will come my workers!

Give up jealousy and conceit. Learn to
work unitedly for others. This is the
great need of our country.

— swami vivekananda

Authors View

When I was in standard 8th I started writing very short lines on different topics that I observed in literature. Yes, this inspiration for writing skill came from the second home of mine St. Aloysius Convent High School, Bhusawal.

From school time, I did not know how to write in a better way. Then I started writing in diaries. I never cared about my grammar, vocabulary, or language of write-ups because I was unaware of professional words and proper literature. But strong desire helped me to go on. I tried to start knowing about literature. I started to build confidence in myself. I started writing everything with my emotions in a daily diary personally. My interest was always in reading more and more books along with listening to stories from my grandma.

According to me if any person in this universe practices, studies and follows the teachings of Chhatrapati Shivaji Maharaja, Chhatrapati Sambhaji Maharaja, Mahatma Phule, Savtrimai Phule, Dr. Babasaheb Ambedkar, Santa Dnyaneshwar, Santa Tukaram, Swami Vivekananda, Dr. APJ Abdul Kalam, and all those great human beings who taught every human to follow humanity. Then he can do anything in his life.

As a student representative from school time helped me a lot to gain experience. By observation and considering the current scenario inspired me to write on Social, Youth, and Nature reformation. According to me, we can include each and every problem faced by youths and generations in these three sectors specifically Social-Youth-Nature. Focusing on youth especially under rural development is necessary. I have tried my level best to highlight some major points and issues creating awareness. I have completed my task as a student and youth of this nation.

The book "The Empowering uniqueness" contains an introduction on various angles of youths and perspective as per my understanding and observation. The Second edition of the book will talk in detail about all problems and solutions from the research point of view.

Although carefully studied and reviewed, this book may contain errors of typography or statement. Any report will be welcomed by the author. The book intends to create awareness and if any mistakes occurred I accept and welcome it to improve my level of understanding and knowledge and assure not to repeat it again.

Ketan V. Firke.

Author

Ketanfirke1112@gmail.com

Acknowledgements

First of all, I appreciate and thank my Parents. I think one of the most precious gifts given by God to me is my Parents. The love of parents is selfless and they sacrifice their happiness for our happiness. No matter how big the children grow, they always remain small for the parents. Any relationship in the world can be false but the relationship between parents and children is always true. Parents always want to see their children succeed and fulfill their needs. Parents are unique, there is no other in the world like them. We should always respect our parents because they meet only once in life. Because of them, I am progressing and I can write and learn. There are no words for you Aai and Baba, Love you.

I especially thank and appreciate all my teachers from time of school, college, coaching, and every person who has taught me and helped me for my intellectual and overall growth till now and who molded me with all-round knowledge. Every person who inspired me to write this book is my inspiration. Thank you So much to everyone.

Special Thanks to Miss Manisha.S.Deshmukh for inspiring me to read more and more books. Manisha mam is one of the best examples of women empowerment and has an all-round personality. Manisha mam is an English teacher, Law Degree holder, Active in politics as Sarpanch of Purnard, and inspiring light to every student along with me.

- To Atal Foundation – Special thanks to Atal Foundation Under the leadership of respected Dr. Sunil Neve Sir working with full pace for Social welfare and Youth encouragement. Your work is really appreciable sir. Atal Foundation specifically works for all the social issues with encouraging activities. Atal Foundation focuses on education and rural development. I especially thank Atal Foundation and Dr. Sunil Neve sir of Jalgaon district for encouraging youths and creating a skillful spark in Students. The best quality of each and every member of the Atal Foundation team is that they are always ready for social welfare programs and reforming activities for students with Leadership. Special thanks to sir for contributing always the best towards Development and their guiding knowledge that enlightens and ignites each and every student.

- To Eco-Indium Welfare activity – Special thanks to Eco INDIUM Welfare activity Under Leadership of Omkar Jagdale, Ketan Firke(Author), Pushpak Chaudhari(Author), Sagar Ugale, Ved Thorat, Tejas Ubale, Siddhi Jagdale, Ashay Sakhare, Samprit Kadam, and the whole team working with desired passion for national welfare and wholeheartedly towards betterment. Eco Indium welfare activity is specifically working on Environment, climate change, agricultural and rural development with Social, Youth and Nature Reformation. This is an activity by the youths for the youths towards National welfare. Free of cost mental peace and meditation workshops, guiding seminars for farmers, free food for roaders, a free medical check-up for tribal and many more programs are arranged by these youths. The Word INDIUM means In National Development of Indian Universal Moment and it is the oath followed by every member. Special Thanks to all our teammates for arranging such programs and providing a great platform towards development and welfare that enriched me with experience and was full of thoughts.

- To Trustworthiness activity – Special Thanks To Trustworthiness team under the leadership of Abhishek Patil and Leena V. Bhangale which is doing a great job for poor people on the road by providing food. The activity also focuses on learning new skills for rural area students in support of eco-indium welfare activity under rural development. May God bless the whole team and may you all continue doing social work for the welfare and development of the nation. Thank you for your support.

Special Thanks to Mayur Bhangale, Nitesh Patil, Mayur Chavan, and Digambar Kumbhar (from Jalgaon district Maharashtra) for managing and contributing to graphics in Social programs and especially for this activity.

I especially thank all my near and dear friends who supported me and inspired me to write this book along with sharing their experiences as teenagers and youths of our nation.

Disclaimer

"The Empowering Uniqueness" is a book proclaiming Social, Youth, and Nature Reformation. The book effectively expresses only the perspective of the author and there is no intention to harm the sentiments of any person. Each and every point written in this book is the author's observation and desire for creating positive awareness. The book is meant for awareness purposes only and we do not intend to hurt the sentiments of any individual, community, sect, or religion. The images used in script are only for creating awareness and credit for the images used belongs to the original creators. This book is a work for highlighting awareness points with personal perspective and any resemblance to any person living or dead is purely coincidental.

Preface

"The Empowering Uniqueness" is uniqueness in you. The further chapters focus on Youth, Social and Environmental aspects.

We know that our country is the fastest growing economy in the world. Our country is soon to become a developed nation. One-fifth of the world's youth live in our nation is the fact. According to my perspective, India's youth population is its most valuable asset and a challenge as well. This provides India with a unique demographic advantage. But without proper investment in capital development, social development, natural development, and most important youth development, this opportunity will be lost. At the same time, today's world is more dynamic and uncertain than ever before. As India undergoes rapid and uniform economic, demographic, social, and technological changes, it must be ensured that its development is inclusive and reaches all sections of the society. India will not be able to realize its true growth potential unless its youth can participate in its economy adequately and productively. The upcoming chapters will provide a wider angle for youths.

Our Young Indians are ambitious and show more autonomy in their career decisions. They understand the changing skill requirements and are eager to pursue higher education, undergo additional training, and engage in skill development programs. At the same time, many factors are coming in the way of their aspirations and preventing them from adjusting effectively to the changing nature of work. I think the youths of our nation could be a message for government policies to ensure an easier way to move from education to economic activity. According to my observation, the influence of family and friends on the career and educational choices of India's youth is waning. Youth are increasingly looking for productive job opportunities and careers that reflect their aspirations. Many youths have to face many hurdles to find the desired and suitable job opportunities. Factors such as disparity of information on employment and skills and lack of guidance in setting appropriate career goals and making employment choices are holding back the Indian youth. Many people believe that they are away from any kind of counselling opportunities. Career counselling and mentoring can help understand the disparity between competence and ambition and can help improve career choices for young Indians. But we lack awareness here.

As the nature of work changed with the Industrial Revolution, existing gender biases are likely to increase if dedicated policies and initiatives are not implemented to address them. Instead of repeating today's prejudices, efforts are needed to reduce them in the field of the future. The proliferation of social media and internet usage amongst India's youth provides opportunities to raise awareness about education pathways, employment opportunities, skill requirements, and available skill development programs. But also ruins the lives of many youths. So consideration of pros and cons is very important.

Several steps are being taken in the right direction, such as the Start-up India initiative of the Government of India to promote entrepreneurship; Launch of Skill India Mission; creating a dedicated Ministry for Skill Development and Entrepreneurship; Establishment of Industry oriented Skill Councils and rejuvenation of Industrial Training Institutes. While such openings indicate that the Indian government is committed to efficiency, this policy is specifically about choice or heritage to understand the youth's preferences for employment and the realities of the market. This gap is likely to widen with changes like jobs and work with the Industrial Revolution. Going forward, the collaboration between various government agencies and ministries, the private sector, academic experts, training organizations, civil society, and youth will be key to harnessing the potential of Young India. Our ability to meet the aspirations of the next generation is critical to promoting labour productivity and inclusive growth. The book focuses on highlighting points along with creating awareness. You will get the different and wide angles in upcoming chapters, so stay tuned, keep smiling, stay calm and keep reading further.

भारत देश तरुणांचा देश आहे. भारताची मोठी ताकद म्हणजे भारतीय तरुण आहेत. याच तरुणांवर अनेक राष्ट्र द्रोही ताकदीचा डोळा आहे .भारतातील मेहनती , जबाबदार राष्ट्रप्रेमी ,निसर्गप्रेमी ,धर्मप्रेमी तरुण नकारात्मक , आळ्सी, व्यसनी कसे होतील अशी प्रयत्न या शक्ती करीत आहेत.अशा शक्तीना रोखून तरुणांमध्ये राष्ट्रप्रेम,निसर्गप्रेम ,सामाजिक समरसता निर्माण करण्यासाठी ताकद येणे संघठीतपणे प्रयत्न करण्याची आवश्यकता आहे.

आज तरुणांमध्ये या गोष्टींविषयी अनेक संशय दिसून येतात किंवा तरुणांमध्ये राष्ट्राच्या उत्थानासाठी जागृतता दिसून येत नाही. स्वास्थ्य ,निसर्ग ,प्रदूषण या समस्यांबाबतीत अनभिज्ञता दिसून येते.आजच्या धावत्या युगाशी स्पर्धा करीत असताना चिडचिडेपणा ,हट्टीपणा ,आत्महत्या ,भांडण असे साईड इफेक्ट तरुणांमध्ये दिसत आहेत अशीच परिस्थिती कायम राहिली तर भविष्यात भयंकर परिणामांना सामोरे जाण्याची वेळ येऊ शकते.यासाठी तरुणांचा आत्मविश्वास वाढवून त्यांना जबाबदारीची जाणीव करुन देणे, त्यांच्याशी प्रेमाने सवांद करणे महत्वाचे आहे.

The Empowering Uniqueness - Towards Social,Youth & Nature Reformation या पुस्तकाच्या माध्यमातून लेखकाने जी प्रयत्न केली आहेत ती कौतुकास्पद आहे. या सर्व टीमला माझ्या शुभेच्छा व भविष्यात अशीच सकारात्मक समाजाच्या निर्माणासाठी प्रयत्न करत राहावेत ही अपेक्षा.

महामंडलेश्वर श्री जनार्दन हरि जी महाराज सतपंथ संतकृपा आश्रम फैजपुर

महाराष्ट्र शासन

जिल्हाधिकारी तथा जिल्हा दंडाधिकारी, जळगाव यांचे कार्यालय,

(स्वीय सहाय्यक कक्ष)

दुरध्वनी क्र : ०२५७२२२०४००. जिल्हा पेठ, आकाशवाणी केंद्राजवळ, जळगाव- ४२५००१.
ई-मेल : collector.jalgaon@maharashtra.gov.in

क्रमांक/स्वीय सहा/ईटपाल/ २०२१/५६/१२७/२९५७   दिनांक -२६/१०/२०२१

प्रति,

श्री केतन विलास फिरके.

विषय : शुभेच्छा पत्र!

आपण दि. २६ ऑक्टोबर, २०२१ रोजी माझी सदिच्छा भेट घेऊन आपण स्वतः प्रकाशित केलेले पुस्तक 'The Empowering Uniqueness' हे पुस्तक भेट दिले, याबद्दल आपले मनःपुर्वक धन्यवाद!

युवक, युवकांचा सामाजिक अडचणी व निसर्गाकडे पाहण्याचा दृष्टीकोन, शैक्षणिक व सामाजिक उन्नती साठी करावयाचे प्रयत्न याबाबतच्या बृहद दृष्टिकोन विशद करणारे पुस्तक प्रसिध्द करणे ही नक्कीच अभिनंदनीय बाब आहे.

आपल्या कार्याला माझ्या मनःपुर्वक शुभेच्छा! आपल्या क्षेत्रात आपण उत्तरोत्तर यशाची शिखरे पादाक्रांत कराल अशी मला आशा आहे. धन्यवाद!

अभिजीत राऊत
जिल्हाधिकारी तथा
जिल्हादंडाधिकारी जळगाव

RAKSHA NIKHIL KHADSE
Member of Parliament
Lok Sabha, Raver (Maharashtra)

Member :
- Standing Committee on Information Technology
- Standing Committee on Welfare of O. B. C.
- Standing Committee on Empowerment of Women
- Consulative Committee onM/o Culture and M/o Tourism
- Board of Governors
  National Institute of Fashion Technology

Delhi:
N-603, "Narmada" New MS Flats
Dr. Bishamber Daas Marg,
New Delhi-110 001
TeleFax : 011-23719733
E-mail : rakshataikhadse@gmail.com

Residence :
At Post Kothali,
Muktainagar-425 306
District Jalgaon (MS)
TeleFax : 02583-235050

Outward.No.:Muk.Offi./**492**/2021
Dated 27th October 2021

**To,
Shri. Ketan Vilas Firke
Book Author – "The Empowering Uniqueness"**

The concept of the book "The Empowering Uniqueness" is very good. Being young student of our nation, your perspective toward society is appreciable.

The topics like budding youth of our nation, new approach toward politics and true empowerment with role in community specifies your leadership quality. We are proud to have youths like you Ketan Firke and Pushpak Chaudhari.

I wish you will build and reform people like you in our society along with rural and national development of our nation needs more people like you.

All the very best for your upcoming journey with agriculture and climate research's models along with your "The Empowering Uniqueness" book.

I am sure this will help the distracted and addicted youth to overcome the challenge faced by them.

May god bless you...!

Yours Well Wisher

Smt. Raksha Nikhil Khadse
Member of Parliament, Raver Lok Sabha

Master Ketan Phirke   Date: 27/10/2021
Navi Tal Yawal Dist Jalgaon

Heartily Congratulations dear Master Ketan Phirke for such a wonderful and well planned, well constructed book at the very tender age. Being an engineering student, you have explored your views in such a beautiful way. You have tried to present the issues related to the present socio-cultural situation of the nation and the expected role of the youngsters As we know that India is the youngest nation in the world. More than 52% population of our nation is young. This young generation is the store house of the extreme energy .

Youths have the ability to reshape and reconstruct the national policy of development by their creativity and ability both the intellectual as well physical. Instead of searching for the government jobs, the youth can create their own place, can work independently. Instead of job seeker, become job giver.

This book has focused very well on the expected role of the youth. You have remarkably presented the expectations from the young generation especially during the pandemic situation.If we look at the medal tally of Tokyo Paralympic 2020, we will realise that if the physicaly disabled youth can bring medals, laurels to the nation; then why can't we who suppose to be fit both physically and mentally.

You have focused on the women empowerment also and that is the prominent feature of this book I must say.* *youngsters as well as the women are the key factors in the process of the nation's overall development.

A nation having the constructive minded, optimistic, enthusiastic yougesters including the male and female will definately reach the height of the progress.
Your efforts are really praisworty.
I must say that every youth has to read this book and think positively to glorify his/her as well as family's name.
I wish best luck for your bright future.

Vishnu Ramdas Bhangale
Ex.Management Council Member
Senate member KBCNMU Jalgaon
Ex-Mayor/Corporator Jalgaon Municipal Corporation.
Shivsena Jilha Pramukh Jalgaon

330, वैष्णवी, ओंकार नगर, जळगाव 425 001 ☐ +91 94222 77177 ☎ 0257 222 9494 ✉ vishnubhangale9999@gmail.com

लालचंद प्रभाकर पाटील

उपाध्यक्ष - जिल्हा परिषद, जळगांव
सभापती - बांधकाम व अर्थ समिती

कार्यालय : दुरध्वनी : (०२५७) २२२९६८७
शासकीय निवास : काव्य रत्नावली चौक, महाबळ रोड, जळगांव, दुरध्वनी : (०२५७) २२६२३७८
निवास : मु.पो. नशिराबाद, ता.जि. जळगाव. फोन : (०२५७) २३५६५९८ मो.नं. ☎ ९४२३७७३४७८

जा.क्र.   दिनांक : 26/ 10 / २०२१

To,
Shri. Ketan Vilas Firke
Book Author – "The Empowering Uniqueness"

Your Book "The Empowering Uniqueness" is appreciable for Youth and for our country. You have explained the concepts in very good way. The understanding level and your intellectual approach is mindblowing.

I wish you and your team team Eco-Indium Welfare the best for working in national welfare. I recommend every youth to read this book. Your work is appreciable and management for social activities is excellent.

The content in your book "The Empowering Uniqueness" will surely help youth public to avoid and come out of addiction. Your works for agriculture and climate change with research concepts is also practical and wish you all the best for that.

May all your dreams come true. May God bless you! Keep working for youths and betterment of our nation with National Welfare.

ALL THE BEST.

Yours well Wisher

(Lalchand Prabhakar Patil)
Vice President
Zilla Parishad, Jalgaon.

179

     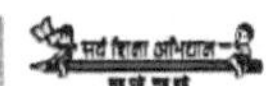

xxix

नेहरु युवा केन्द्र जलगाँव
Nehru Yuva Kendra Jalgaon

जिला कार्यालय
नेहरु युवा केन्द्र संगठन
स्वायत्तशासी संस्था
युवा कार्यक्रम एवं खेल मंत्रालय
भारत सरकार

District Office of the
Nehru Yuva Kendra Sangathan
an Autonomous Body under the
Ministry of Youth Affairs & Sports
Government of India

MESSAGE

Youth of any nation has the immense potential to change its destiny. So, India being a nation of youth, can be the world's 3rd largest economy well in advance. However, the significant number of youth in India is inadvertently moving on the wrong path which can be avoided with collaborative actions of the Government and civil societies.

All the issues which are narrated by the **Young Authors** are very much relevant to the present scenario and the holistic and practical way forwards mentioned in the book are also very impressive. The book depicts the authors' observation, foresight and vision. It is a matter of pride for me to be a part of this book which is a reflection of society.

All the best.

(Narender)
District Youth Officer

गट नं. ४०, प्लॉट नं. ६०, द्रौपदी नगर, जलगाँव – 425001
Gat No. 40, Plot No. 60, Draupadi Nagar, Jalgaon - 425001
Phone : 0257 - 2951754   Email : qnykjalgaon@gmail.com

आ. सुरेश दामू भोळे (राजूमामा)
विधानसभा सदस्य (जळगांव शहर)
मो. ९४२२२७७२४२. mail: mlasureshdbhole@gmail.com

DATE: - 26/10/2021

To,

Shri Ketan Vilas Firke,

Author - "The Empowering Uniqueness".

"The Empowering Uniqueness" book is amazing and I wish every youth to go through these points. The topics in this book are fascinating and specially the novel approach towards politics section. The points you make in the book are socially important and are meant to inspire the younger generation to do social work and awareness.

I have gone through major topics mentioned in your book and I analyzed that you have tried to show the Youth the strength of the Youth of our Nation, specifically points on the education system and the youth. Today's young generation really needs to think about those issues and it is very commendable work that you are conveying this book to the youth.

You are conveying very beautiful message. May God bless you...! Shri Ketan Firke and Shri Pushpak Chaudhari with your eco-indium welfare activity team.

All The Best with 'The Empowering Uniqueness' book and upcoming book releases!

Your's

S - D.

MLA Suresh Bhole (Rajumama)

The Empowering Uniqueness – Towards Social Youth And Nature Reformation

This book is sun-rays to the youths who have lost their hopes & ambitions. It is an awakening call for youth to serve our nation through different fields.

An oath starts the journey from pre-maturity to maturity which leads to a perfect & successful person towards a nation builder. An author himself is aware of his strength & capacity, with strong determination & confidence, he explained each and every winning strategy of youth. It is an inspirational & motivational book for every person.

The writer keenly wants to empower the youth, so he used his imagination into writing skill. An inner urge of young man speaks about the welfare of society as well as the nation. The writer effectively used his hand, head, and heart for this book. This book travels from Upanishads- Puranas to Artificial intelligence. The writer reflects his own experiences, thoughts, and ideas positively to show the right path for young generation. The writer tried to give best ideas. Definitely promisingly career & innovative World is waiting for the writer.

ALL THE BEST.

Prof. Advt. Manisha Sandeep Deshmukh

M. A. B. Ed. LLB

SARPANCH, Purnard, Jalgaon

To,

Mr. Ketan Vilas Firke

The facts in the book "The Empowering Uniqueness" are very reliable and need to be focused on them. The content like youth leadership, youth's role in development of nation and politics is main attraction of your book.

The idea of connecting to problems of youth's nature & difficulties is appreciable & effective. Awareness raising is very powerful, because it educates people about topics which are new to them and encourages to participate in bringing students like you Ketan Firke & Pushpak Chaudhari who came forward to make awareness about bad addictions and problems faced by the youths.

As a student and a youngster you have done a great effort of spreading awareness through your book in today's youth. The youth is the hope of our future. I will recommend every youth to read this book and think about what they can do to make our nation proud on them.

I wish you all the best for "The Empowering Uniqueness" & your upcoming projects &journey.

May God Bless You.

Shri. Dr. Sunil Neve Sir.

(Social Worker &

President of Atal Foundation)

Personally my opinion about "The Empowering Uniqueness" book is that the author has covered all different topics with awareness touch in this book. The vision of author is so wide that not a single subject is left over for youngsters and everything is covered with proper awareness. The benefit of this book is that if someone have not seen any book about youths or have not studied anything related to Social, Youth and Nature parameters then also by this book he can grasp basically everything for reformation and development. Only readers need to focus and concentrate on every subject of this book. Nowadays youths are getting matured very early, if we look at past many years before youngsters were getting proper matured after age of 22 and 23 and now maturity comes from age of 15 and 16. Ketan V. Firke is the best example for this. In such small age author has come out with such huge concept that can be compared with 40 years of experience. Proud of you youngsters and May god bless you child. All the best for your future.

Shri. Gani Meman
(Social Activist, Maharashtra)

Todys time for India is going through revolutionary phase. For that the foundation of young generation, youths and society should be very strong. Youths play very crucial role in such scenario. As we all know that India is called as nation full of youth so nation building is only possible by the initiative of youths in our country. The topics covered by author with science towards reformation creates the mindset and provides vibes of real power of youths. In nation Building basically youths are only the best factor that can change toxic mindsets with changing traditional old methods. Socioeconomic development can be done and the gap between high and low classes can be reduced says this book, also with technology and rural development and that is only possible by youths of country with intellectual mindsets. I appreciate author and recommend every youth to read this book once. Awareness creating content is required for socioeconomic and overall development of our young generation. May god bless you and all the best.

Shri. Vinayak Phalak.
(Young Entrepreneur)

Empowering youth is the best book I have read it gives the exact idea of what exactly youth is facing. If everyone read this book, definitely it will make big evolution in our society. Also, I thank our author Ketan V. Firke for publishing this book.

Shri. HG. Deshmukhe.
(Prahar Janshakti Party -
Student Vice President, Yawal)

The book "Empowering Uniqueness" is reformation for Youths of our nation and all scenarios are related to young generation. As a youth of this nation I recommend every youth to read this book. LIFE CHANGING BOOK .So teenagers can read this book for making improvements in their life and also it will make huge changes in their life. May god bless you author Ketan Firke and all the best for future.

Shri. Prithviraj Ravi Patil
(Social Activist & Vice President
Amature Sports Kick Boxing
Association District Jalgaon)

{Thank you so much to each and every person from my mentors, guides, youths and student community members reviewed for our book, "The Empowering Uniqueness". I am blessed and happy to have people like you all with me. Dear readers my prayers and good wishes are there with every one of you. Due to limitation of space it is not possible to add each and every person's review here, but I accept it respectfully and thank you all with bottom of my heart.}

SECTION-1

A. The Budding Youths of Nation - Strategic Novelty towards Every Sunshine.

Being Youthful.

"We cannot always build the future of the youth, but we can build the youth for the future", Franklin Roosevelt. This statement which is quoted for us depends on us. It is really a fact. If the present generation of the youth is not familiar with their responsibilities towards the society or the nation, they are at loss. A loss isn't a financial or social loss, it is the self-recognition loss, a loss of their status, and a loss of their esteem. The distraction counts in the millennium, there's not a single reason for it. The word 'YOUTH' holds a deep meaning one should know:

Y: Young and Versatile warrior of the country should be:

O: Optimistic NOT Pessimistic
U: United NOT Divided
T: Trustworthy NOT Falsehood
H: Honest AND NOT A Forced Liar.

This year marks the 75th independence of our motherland, we call it "Azadi ka Amrut Mahotsav". Yeah! Externally it is a proud moment for the country to celebrate the dignity and pride of our motherland. But do we think? What about the youths of the same nation, who had been distracted with their aims? Why aren't they getting back in their normal which was disturbed during pandemics and lockdowns? Everyone was locked, everything was closed but not all opportunities were locked. Rather the lockdown was the best period for all the youths to enrich their productive time enthusiastically. But we never looked beyond all those activities related to social media. We wasted the days making our body focused on only one aspect or the only CHOICE and that was spending the whole day on social media. Didn't that made us a meaningful person or a useless one? Today we regret, regret killing ourselves, and regret the time we passed, the enthusiasm we wasted, and most importantly the opportunities we lacked. This all never mattered a year back but matters now. A student will have millions of things to do if he has the desire to do it. Otherwise, it's all for the show-off. Neither the parents know nor any other group what's the actual desire we have is the reality. It is only our inner voice that knows everything about us and within us. Research and innovation along with Social, Youth, and Natural awareness are most necessary for our youth's life. We know that it is a science age, you can also say that it is a digital age. The past old world and today's modern world are now very different. Only science and technology have changed this world, we will see that in upcoming chapters for you readers. Due to the COVID effect in the world, every student is stuck up to Techeducation and social media. The world is so close to students but we can see many positive and negative aspects of it as well. In our world, most of our colleagues, schools, and organizations are organizing research activities for the student. Because they want to develop students' skills and creativity. Why do they want to organize these things? You will get a novel approach in this chapter THE BUDDING YOUTHS OF NATION - STRATEGIC NOVELTY TOWARDS EVERY SUNSHINE. My youths –the world is yours. Wake up and start working, struggle till the end, be strong, put effort, and everything you wish is yours. Stay calm and stay in tune with the Novel perspective for you in this chapter. You can read every moral headline and follow it along with creating awareness and empowerment. So, dear beloved, Along with the passing 75th year of independence of INDIA, can't we make a resolution to make ourselves a better living person and a warrior who can contribute to the nation? I guess it's time for this generation to be self-reliant and decision-makers, one who firmly believes that perfect youth and perfect youth mentality will surely reach till heights of reformation. This creativity is most important to get a way of success and work for welfare empowering youth reformation. We just need to decide dear reader and you can be the Change-maker. Let us start this chapter with the youthful sunshine.

● **Youthful Sunshine 1: Take Resolution to Contribute For Betterment of Nation.**

People make resolutions to bring the required changes in their lifestyles which might improve themselves.

Let us take a resolution oath, today readers.

On a personal level, almost everyone takes some promises, but we should not forget the fact that it is our Motherland that matters the most. Hence, some resolutions must also be taken to make our nation a better place.

Let us make a resolution to keep our country clean, maintain Cleanliness in society and environment and will keep our country as clean as heaven.

Let us make a resolution to minimize the corruption. Every small step we take matters in the long run.

Let us make our nation corruption-free.

Let us make a resolution to improve education quality and system by being practical with not depending more on theory.

The exposure to different disciplines is less. Still a trend of RAT RACE is followed, isn't it? We will change it to contribute every small step towards improving the literacy and education ranking of our nation on top.

It is due to poverty that uncountable hungry stomachs sleep at night.

Rich are getting richer, poor are getting poorer. Poverty is the consequence of less education, illiteracy, corruption, lack of Opportunities, discrimination, etc.

So, let us make a resolution to eradicate poverty by in return eradicating the factors which cause them.

Let us make our country a better place to sustain Happily, Healthy, and successfully.

● **Youthful Sunshine 2: Make Your Choices The Best.**

My dear readers, our life is full of confusion at every step, such as what to wear or eat, what to follow for our life to change, such as what career to select? Whether to get married, if yes then to whom, what profession to take, and many more. In a hurry, excitement, curiosity, and jealously we put on our right to choose spontaneously, and yes sometimes we make bad decisions that are useless leave us full of regret.

What we have to do is, do not fear the consequences going to happen if we are on the right path. The worst might never happen and if it does you have the psychological inner voice guiding you.

It makes us think, to make good choices or decisions you need time to think about all the good and bad aspects of various alternatives, but sometimes a snap instinctive choice is just as good, if not better.

Keep your aim in front.

Don't cry about past situations.

Let us look towards every choice with an intellectual mind-set. Limit your choices by being aware of social pressure and making your choices the best.

● **Youthful Sunshine 3: Humanity & Mankind.**

I am pleased to see that there are people who are so selfless for the nation. As a youth, less but with experience, I can tell you that time heals wounds. I commend to your heart all the questions of Human welfare and mankind.

You have time in front of you now and major serious tasks, to bring up your lovely children with humanity and to finish up the work you started.

Let them be the main content of your life.

Because you cannot change the world, but you can start the concept of looking forward towards betterment.

Aim to increase our love of volunteering my youth from an early age by providing a variety of volunteer opportunities.

Go and work with organizations, NGOs, develop welfare activities, work for social issues with your required intellectual growth, work for natural welfare and environmental sustainability, work towards human resources and try your best for its development.

I am of the clear mindset that if you are not getting any opportunity, you be the one.

You are Youths of the world and every youth has the potential to create the change and to be the change.

Start your work for Humanity.

This is the correct time for you. Don't waste a minute just Start with the concept you have in your mind.

All the best.

● Youthful Sunshine 4: Create Your Own System

My dear reader, you are the creator of your own life.

Always there is uniqueness in every person. Even you have that uniqueness, just you are blind to see it. What you need to do is open your eyes and keep working, then the whole world is yours. But open your eyes from the internal source of your soul. Create your own style of work and it will lead to creating your system for welfare and your intellectual growth.

● Youthful Sunshine 5: Do You Know Yourself?

I will say you to be comfortable with yourself. Always remember, "You laugh at me because I'm different. I laugh at you because you're all the same." Some people copy each other because they don't have their own style.

Be unique and people will love you. Staying in control will help you to become the person you want to be.

Act normal. Don't try to be perfect. Be assertive and accept yourself.

Feel the change. Start applying your plans and be the game-changer.

● Youthful Sunshine 6: Extra Natural Powers You Have.

Dear reader, Youths have so much potential that if they use it in constructive work they can lead the nation on a path of success and if they use it in destructive work they may destroy the nation with their own life.

Believe in your powers and everything is yours of which you wish off.

Try your best to overcome negatives, focus on your internal power and you will get introduced to the Superhero and that superhero is you, my dear reader.

Don't think of others, don't waste time, and just start your way.

● Youthful Sunshine 7: Set Your Goal And Grow Your Future.

What are your goals? The resolutions include exercising more, quitting all bad habits like smoking, learning a new skill, managing money better, etc.

Psychology says the goal-setting key is to listen to yourself and focus on the process of improvement rather than the product.

Your aim holds the promise of helping you in many parts of your output, and I will recommend you to look beyond academics.

When youth are overscheduled and stressed, you need to identify goals and action steps that help in relaxation and fun as part of life.

I have experienced it. Every step you take should be towards your goal and then there is no power to stop you from growing your future.

Youthful Sunshine 8: Poverty Can Change Your Destiny.

Are you poor? But by the mind. The thought of money is never far away from everyone. In fact, just as you focus on your name poorer people might tune into the finances of things more readily.

Poorer people look at money-related things were more likely than wealthier people say that "money" is in the things. Income didn't appear to affect how people respond to others.

So Poverty is a mind-set.

Take everything as a challenge. Let us change our mind-set and destiny is yours. But you cannot make reasons about conditions that are not favourable for me.

Just remember you are the creator of yourself and you can create anything in any unfavourable conditions

● Youthful Sunshine 9: Do You Know About Self-Esteem?

Self-Esteem means self-respect. The respect of yourself. We can say it as a realistic, appreciative opinion of oneself. Dear reader,

Realistic means we're dealing in the verity, being directly and actually apprehensive of our strengths, Sins, and everything in between.

Appreciative, still, suggests that we've good passions overall about the person we see.

Suppose of a friend who knows you well and cherishes you, entertain there's further to you than your faults, and you'll get a sense of what appreciative means.

There's no need to be arrogant or boastful, no need to suppose that we are more worthwhile as a person than others or further professed or important than we really are.

Indeed, it is a strong motivator to work hard. Accept it and move on.

● **Youthful Sunshine 10: Be Aware For Being Youthful and Meaningful.**

Our life and our perception of externals can change the way we feel about ourselves. The awful news, still, is that we can learn how to develop self-esteem. If we consider awareness then, Awareness contemplation has been planted in recent times to ameliorate a wide range of medical and cerebral conditions, ranging from habitual pain to stress, anxiety, depression, sleep diseases, and eating diseases. It appears to increase exertion in the area of the brain associated with happiness and Sanguinity. Interpreters of awareness frequently feel more tone- confident and comfortable in their own skin despite external events. In fact, results have been so emotional that awareness contemplation is now being tutored in academic medical centres, pain conventions, hospitals, and seminaries including law seminaries all over the world.

●**Youthful Sunshine 11: Deleting Unnecessary Things Can Save You.**

Avoid all unwanted things taking you to destroy yourself.

Technology, Procrastination, Disorganization, Multitasking, Lack of Sleeping time, checking how many followers counts on social media, girlfriend, boyfriend, sex, porn, comparing past with others, being obsessed, jealousy, extra anger, winning every argument, being busy without reason, blaming others, having fun all the time, criticizing yourself, bragging, having a constant fear of missing out, spending time with toxic people, appearing smart, etc.

If you delete all the irrelevant things according to the individual's unnecessary requirements then it can save you.

Learn to unlearn some drawbacks you have in yourself and experience the power.

B. Why There Is Need Of Youth Empowerment & Awareness?

As the young people of our nation, reader, you are at the focused point of absolute strength. You have big potentials, there is no stopgap for the betterment, and can have a vision about a better future, and thus making nonstop sweats to turn your dreams into reality should be our purpose. We can say that youth empowerment is a process where people focus and achieve the ability with authority to make thoughtful and informed decisions that can implement to create change. It is actually a mean for youth encouragement to do things of success and achieve sky heights for themselves and also for creating a great impact in their society. I think Youth Empowerment is a process, to encourage youth by every capable source. Only youths can get involved and can be change-makers. Being practical, it is trouble towards making a course for youths to sustain and acclimatize as per the situations. It aims at perfecting the quality of life, youth are living and bringing accreditation by giving them access to the coffers which can help them to make confidence and work in the direction of attaining progressive growth, intellectual growth, and a contributor in national welfare. There are fruitful and encouraging programs that are launched to empower youth in different verticals.

The programs are run either by NGOs, Government Organizations or Activities such as Eco- Indium Welfare (National Development of Indian Universal Moment) by the Government College of Engineering and Research College Awsari, Pune students in Maharashtra, or the programs organized by the youths for the youth, all these can lead to national welfare.

Dear reader, you have a great opportunity to contribute to national welfare. Wake up and start it your way. Youth authorization focuses on creating a better community and creating a strong independent existent. The youth delegation conditioning is addressed towards making a gateway to personality development, transnational equity, Civic Engagement, and republic structure. Majorly it contributes towards national development, so why not you be a part of it? Youth mandate will help to make a better hereafter which elevates the standard of living of the people. It is pursued by promoting youth rights, youth activism, social activism, nature activism, and standing for the right. It inculcates values in individualities to make them a better standing existent. It is the most effective way to make a better future for our country. India is a country bulging in youth. Around many people below the age of 40 are suffering from hard times. While an estimate of 34 to 35% of India's Gross National Income is contributed by the youth; there's a dire need to develop this chance. Actually, it is an opportunity. In fact, the youth moment is a major resource for not only the development of fiscal substance but for social changes as well. Despite holding similar significance, they frequently face hurdles, with their energy still not being canalized in the right direction. This challenge isn't confined to the Government, but also the entire private section in the country. The need for youth empowerment and encouragement is related, to the fiscal elevation and also proliferation of the standard of living. Mindfulness is a crucial factor, with guidance towards developing a wholesome outlook of life. Youth Reformation in any development is imperative not only for the public development of an entire country but also for the particular development of an existent. Youth Reformation is pursued by promoting youth rights, promoting youth activism, and in community decision.

Reformation is inescapably a process of inculcating values to equip the learner to lead a life that's satisfying to the existent while agreeing with the cherished values and ideals of the society. At present, it's the most effective means that society possesses for defying the challenges of the future. Then we can observe there are many reasons, why Youth empowerment is essential? For Poverty, eradication Youth can help to reduce the rate of poverty to a significant position. The best key to empowering youth is through skill development. When a youth is equipped with essential chops, he can use them to feed, help others, and indeed invest for unborn use, abetting the nation economically. This will indirectly contribute towards betterment and increase in employability that adds to the GDP of the nation. Good education standards can help youth to understand the significance of education that leads to the social enhancement of the country. Don't you feel that it is really a need? When a youth is empowered, he understands the significance of education and helps hoist the sector, integral for a developing nation similar to India. Similar empowered youth can contribute educational installations to primary, secondary, and indeed to tertiary institutions. According to current observation, India lacks the proper structure for education, which can fluently be brought into actuality only through commission. Good governance with the inculcation of youth development with help of commission, the youth can reject the status quo and pave a path for a better future. At the moment, the youth is claiming his right to a decent living by being willing to take pitfalls, which helps in the development of leadership chops. In other words, to make a better hereafter, we need to nurture the saplings of the moment. Hence, a radical government, which is pro-people, comes from employing bright minds able of taking the nation into a brighter future. Crime reduction Commission ensures that youth has the necessary skill to sustain a livelihood, precluding him to borrow the path of crime.

Presently, a lot has been spent in the name of fighting crime without understanding that the crime affects youth actually in a natural position. It is easy for a youthful impressionable mind to get waylaid and get entangled in anti-social conditioning because he wasn't empowered innocently, academically as well as financially. There are serious social and profitable consequences associated with not addressing the youth who's at the threat of negative circumstances – not only for the youth himself and his family but also for the society at large. I think we together can enable a youthful mind to separate the wrong from the right, denouncing the path of injustice for a respectable living. In today's world and age, youthful minds should have access to coffers to transfigure their knowledge through their beliefs, values, and stations. Don't you think then only we can do it? Can we make our nation "shine", indeed in times of adversity? When the young generation of our nation is empowered, then it can empower at a very mass level, creating a better path for a better future. To build a better tomorrow, we need to nurture the youths of today with the best governance system. What is your opinion on this? Creating employment and employability is another sign of youth empowerment. A youth empowered society won't seriously suffer from the problem of severance that numerous nations are battling within the current time. A skillful youth is and can be a job creator. Not only job creator but also the main contributor of National Economy.

After considering all the aspects. Don't you think there is a need for the nation to create youth awareness? Just think more deeply my reader. Don't you think there is a need for the nation to create Youth Empowerment? Are we going in the right direction? If yes, Are we with the expected pace towards progress? Don't you think there is a need for youths to come into politics? Is it not our responsibility to save our Environment? Is it not our responsibility to save our motherland? We need to develop intellectual thinkers as officers and politicians of our nation. If we are successful in creating such a structure for our nation. The development will become the fact of our motherland.

Due to the limitation of time and space in this book as a youth of this nation and a student of the current system, I am trying to give a different perspective for you readers. It can help you in many aspects of your life as a youth by mind and actions – not by age, so every concept mention is valid for any age group readers. The second edition of the book will talk about the detailed structure. Stay tuned dear reader, Have patience, stay calm, you can win the world. Let us start and continue to read with the next chapter.

C. POWER OF YOUTH – HOW TODAY'S YOUTH SHOULD BE?

Friends, this is my first Activity of writing a book. This book is one of the major activities from the beginning time of mine as a YOUTH and specifically, as a student, all the people who inspired me to write this book are my inspiration. I am writing this book but I'm not a writer with a lot of intelligence. I am writing each and every word with experience, observation, and burning desire for creating something useful and highlighting required perspectives for youth. Have you ever thought, How today's youth should be? Writing about young people does not mean that young people are always disoriented or spoiled. My perspective and tendency is a bit different about this. The chapter will speak about it in a better way.

Whenever we talk about Youth automatically we relate and think about the great person "Swami Vivekananda" and his passion for youth. He is an ideal guru. Today's youth is going to decide the state and direction of tomorrow, but there are many who seduce the youth and abuse them. The process of personal development and social development is an ongoing process. It requires powerful and meditative thinking, isn't it? Youth is the most important and energetic portion of the population in any country. It is believed that developing countries with large youth populations could see tremendous growth, also they invest in young generation's education, health, and safeguarding and guarantee their rights. We can really say that in these days youths are hereafter's originators, generators, builders and leaders. But they need the required support in terms of good health, education, training, and openings to transfigure the future. The economic boost happens when a county's more hands to work available than further mouths to feed. To put it shortly, the working-age population has to be larger than the dependent population. The youth of the moment is decreasingly getting restless and floundering to remove the difference. Still, further sweats need to be put in, if we're to come free from the vicious circles of poverty, malnutrition, corruption, violence, and severance. We can see that all these factors are still in the current situation in society, which really do not allow our great nation to serve in its real spirit.

Unfortunately, being a popular nation and the largest republic in the world, India is still lagging behind in achieving socio-political and profitable equivalence, which were conceived by our forerunners. We the Youth of our nation need to take the charge and come forward to fight against multiple inequalities and contribute to nation-building. India has the edge of the demographic tip is the fact. We have the power to change the nation and if united can create a new world. A youthful mind will be more fresh and innovative which helps in the progress of the country. But acceptable openings should be given to the youth to represent their ideas and programs for the upliftment of the nation. I think the only way to express the ideas and to apply their programs is politics and Economy. Young and intellectual people should be motivated to take part in politics and to enthrall the high positions similar as Prime Minister, Chief Minister and Governor, Officers and young TATA and AMBANI brands. Knowledge and continuity speak a lot rather than experience. For case, a mass kick by the youth in Delhi for justice of Nirbhaya case, a mass kick in Delhi for India against Corruption, and a mass kick in the Marina sand for Jallikattu, etc are some of the prominent exemplifications for the strength of youth. However, also surely India will become an advanced nation soon. If the ruling power is given in the hands of the youth. Youth is only the power and I think it should be encouraged to consider politics as one of the best ways to serve the nation. They should be acquainted with anti-corruption drives with a focus on education, and strategies for fighting corruption. The vital part of the youth who are anew with ideas and not ideals will help in this movement towards a transparent civil society structure which can impact the political administration for the benefit of the society. The only best way is through a strong system of representation that republic work and another best way is only through a strong youth representation that the energy and vigor of a country be maintained. Our country is in great need to resolve most of our problems. Presently India is facing a lot of challenges, and youth are able to work on them. Our youths only need a chance to prove ourselves, If we are not getting it, learn to create it. Individualities are fighting against each other because of the complexion of their skin and the texture of their hair. Religion is another issue, the youths can move their fellow man to live in peace and love. All of us are one and we shouldn't allow these little differences to push us down from each other. Crime is another major factor taking place at a very high level. Women are being killed by their husbands. Person's homes, businesses, are being broken. All such demoralizing activities, crimes, and violence should be given a long break and stopped till the end. The youth formerly more can bring about a change in the country.

Although today's youth are "smart" and have a more or less clear sense of their own personality, it is not only career, money, luxurious life that is important for this personality to flourish, but also thinking about what is happening around them and one's role. This is being ignored by the youth. The country cannot be smart if this is ignored. Youths seem to have the capability to face any issues and challenges. They have a positive influence on their fellow youthful people. They're suitable to educate them about the positive effects in life. The bones who are destroying their future, tend to hear to their fellow youths. They will make them understand the significance of being a good human being. The wise youth that we've out there should be taken into consideration. Some of them, however, educated are jobless. They should be given an occasion to expose their intelligence to the world and make themselves into someone. Government, Civil Society, voluntary organizations, and other stakeholders should help the youths; so that they can make our land a great and educated one. Youths are the power and will for sure make a big difference in society and nation. The youth are our life and nation's pride. They will make our country proud. The country will be honoured. The youth just need the support and enabling terrain at the family position, community position, society position, state position, public position, and transnational position which in turn will them to perform their duties. The part of the youth in the national structure is pivotal.

Friends, what goes but does not come back is youth! That is why all young people should take advantage of every opportunity, accept our next challenges. Young people should be physically, mentally, intellectually, and morally strong, and prosperous. Good people can't be imported, they have to be made. That is why this country has no way out without the youth. The hands of the youth are not for raising but for raising. Dr. Babasaheb Ambedkar

says, "Self-confidence is the key to success." Young people need to awaken their self-confidence. Those whose self-confidence is awakened can achieve success in life. All their money is in vain. If I get a handful of confident people, I will develop this country.
"

Dear readers, the development of the country, the times to come, and the difficulties that arise depend on today's youth. That is why today's youth should be straightforward and wise. Young people should be aware of what the past was like, what the present is like, and what the future will be like. The youth should come together to create a new world by curbing the hypocrisy, stereotypes, corruption, and bad habits in society. The lives of young people should have a goal. The goal must be focused, so that disaster does not occur. They must work hard to achieve the goal. The symptoms of youth are described in the Upanishads. Yuvasyat: Sadhu, Yuvadhyasak: Blessings, determination, strength. A young monk should be straightforward, sincere, pure, and playful. He should be able to accept success without bowing down, and failure without giving reasons. The young man who understands why to live and why to die. Friends, do not go on an addictive diet. Addiction is the greatest enemy of man. Control your senses. Young people, students should have qualities. All you have to do is seek knowledge, devotion, perseverance, concentration, ambition, and so on. Martyr Bhagat Singh once said, "Youth is the spring of human life. The attainment of youth makes a person unconscious". If he decides (as a youth) he can do anything ...Of course, Great Bhagat Singh says it seems true, the youth need change to make the country prosperous. So it is true that politics is becoming young here. And now it seems to us young people that it is wrong and sometimes it is right. They are getting less. The root of that desire is not left today. That is why if you want to make a change, you have to make it yourself first. So in the case of young people, 'Change is the evidence of life, you need to change to make something strong'.

What should be the youth intended for Swami Vivekananda? He says, I want young people who are strong-minded, thoughtful and cultured, who love the nation, the society, who will empower my nation, my society, and my mother India, once again to the pinnacle of that world and on the day when such patriotic youth meet freedom fighters, revolutionaries and many others have said. That is why they say '....Arise! Awake! And stop not till the goal is reached 'I mean get up! Wake up! And don't wait until the goal is achieved. Swami Vivekananda repeatedly reminded the youth of the thoughts that inspire them to live and inspire them to fight. That is why today's youth must assimilate the thoughts of Swami Vivekananda and all the great meditative personalities of INDIA. Thomson Huxley says, "Give me a young man who is physically fit, possesses his desires and vices, his mind is transparent and clear as a mirror; So I will do any miracle in the world. "Today's youth need ideal thinking and skillful leadership and to show the way to the "confused" youth. Everywhere today different parties and other organizations exist under different names only in name. The participation of these organizations is very low for the betterment of society and in fact, such organizations are often used for selfish ends and to divide society. Looking at today's political, social, mental, and economic situation, it seems to me that the responsibility of guiding the youth and creating skilled leadership and perfect person from them really belongs to the people's representatives, social workers, teachers, journalists, and activists. Because if the country's strongest youth are kept ineffective, without leadership, and without direction, then tomorrow's picture will be more complicated than today's. Today's youth thinks differently, his mentality is global! Be Practical. This is the class that says Be particular, but so it is important not to follow anyone blindly and we also pay attention to the happenings in the society with open eyes and take an active part in social work and inspire future generations by creating an ideal. Today's youth is, and should be, "smart", but the difference between smartness and sparkle must also be recognized. Today, being "photogenic" does not work, but only if you are talented, you will get priority and this is the reality. Many educated youths do not even have names on the voter list and this advantage is being widely exploited through fake voting. We can say it abusing. In a youth country like India, the current socialism and politics do not seem to reflect the youth, which costs the country and the city. So far, various changes have been taking place and the youth have made positive use of the various changes that have taken place in the current situation. These young people are seen fulfilling their social commitment through their work. These young people are doing their duty through their art and business. The share of such youth in the revolutionary changes that are taking place in the society is really appreciable and contributing great.

Dear reader, if you have not participated in any kind of reformation, yes this is a chance for you. Come forward and share a great portion towards the betterment of society, humanity, the Environment, and mankind. You are YOUTH- is your POWER. Yes, you have that potential in you, you can change the world towards betterment. Believe in yourself and think about it.

D. EDUCATION SYSTEM AND YOUTHS

Education is a factual process of literacy and acquiring knowledge. Education is authentically important for us because education is the amazing key to mortal success. Education teaches us morality and virtue. The economic and social status of any human being depends largely on his education. So the country that has further educated people, the frugality of that country is also genuinely strong. At the same time, the education system of that country should be good, only then that country becomes powerful in every way. Gurukul was the system of education in ancient times in India. At that time the place of education was in the Gurukul of the forests away from the villages and cities and it was conducted by the sages. The Nalanda and Takshashila schools of India were also similar. The education system of India was so good at that time that foreigners also came to get an education in these schools. In these schools, students had to go to the guru's ashram to take the education of various subjects. And until he completed his education, he had to stay in the ashram with his guru. Along with this, the students had to do their own work. The biggest advantage of this to the students was that the ego in them was completely eliminated. In this way, the education system of ancient India was very tremendous. When India was enslaved by the British, they started erasing the Gurukul system. Lord Thomas Babington Maui Cowley brought the modern education system to India in 1830. In this, the British established schools following a different education system. Apart from this, subjects like Science, Mathematics, and English were brought in unnecessary subjects like Tattvamasa, Darshan and Upanishads taught in Gurukuls. These subjects were quite different from those taught in Gurukuls. Due to all this, there was a sudden change in the education system of India and the attention of the students shifted from the ancient education system to the modern education system of the British. It was really not a good chance for us is the fact. But one thing was very good with the education system of the British that girls also started taking education in it comparing the past time and started going to schools. But we did not get many benefits from the modern education system of the British, because the British had adopted this education system for their benefit. When India became independent on August 15, 1947, the attention of our freedom fighters first went to the modern education system of the British. Because the modern education system of the British was not favorable for our country. Therefore, it was decided to create a new education system in India, in which many committees like the All India Education Committee and Basic Education Committee were formed. Everything in the world needs to change from time to time. Because unless there is a change in something, that thing becomes old at a time. And the things around us move ahead of us.

Similarly, no major changes were made in the education system of India, due to which our education system is considered very weak in today's modern era. That is why Abdul Kalam sir had said that there is a need to completely reform the Indian education system. But we haven't changed it to date. Whereas many developed countries of the world change the curriculum taught in their school every 2 years. But in India, our curriculum has become very old due to a lack of change. This does not mean that our history should not be known to the students of the country. But some practical topics should be included in the syllabus which can be useful in the life of the students. We have a 19th-century curriculum, a 20th-century education system, and 21st-century students. Thus there is a huge difference between the curriculum and the modern students. That is why our students lag behind in every field of the world.

Apart from this, there are two types of education systems in India, government and private. In this, if we talk about government schools, except in some states, the condition of government schools in most of the states is very bad. The main reason for this is that there are two different parties in the state government and the central government. Because of which the synergy between these two is not good. But it harms the students. According to our observation, students in India enrolled in class-1 is less than half of them applying for jobs. Our method of teaching is very old almost everywhere except some top universities like IIm, IIt and some famous institutions. A teacher comes into the classroom and teaches from the book and at the end of the year, the student is assessed. On the basis of that, the future of the student is decided. In our country, the ability of students to memorize is appreciated and the intelligence of the students is judged from the three-hour paper. Nothing to do with their practical abilities here. But this not only spoils the future of the students but also increases the exam stress among the students. Estimate 1 student commits suicide every 1 hour in India today due to rising tension cannot be ignored. For example, a child killed his own friend to postpone his examination in a school and 4 students committed suicide by jumping into a well due to failure in the monthly examination of the school. If this is not the fault of our education system then what is it? Explaining the meaning of education, Gandhiji said that education means the development of physical, mental, and moral powers in children. Not to make them bookworms. But looking at the present education system of India, there is a lot of need for us to improve it. For this, we have to first focus on the skill development of the students and stop giving importance to their marks and ranks. We have to think about how to enhance the cognitive and creative thinking of the students.

Apart from this, practical knowledge is very important for us to develop a deep understanding of any subject. But the present education system of India is focused on theoretical knowledge.

We should change this and adopt practical wisdom. Along with this, we should also change our syllabus according to the time, because our syllabus is the same for decades. As in the present era of computer, so in today's time computer subject should be one of the main subjects in schools and not extra. It is also very important to have good teaching staff, to give good education to the students of the country. But many educational institutions of our country hire teachers who do not have any special experience and skills to teach students to save some money. Such teachers spoil the future of the students by taking less salary. Our educational institutions have to change this approach. Only then can we improve our current education system. We also have to give importance to arts, sports and other activities for the all-round development of the students. Because a man should not depend only on education to be successful in life. If we adopt all these things then perhaps we can improve the present education system. In view of all these things, it is very important for us to bring changes in the basic infrastructure and content of the education system of the country. Only then can we stop such incidents in the country. We can see the majority of youths of our nation India are going abroad because of the faculty, facility, opportunities, infrastructure, and many more things which are lacking in India and the education system, isn't it? Students prefer to learn abroad because they feel there are many opportunities and luxurious life there. Isn't it a very big problem? That is the major reason we and our nation should focus to empower the country with mother's milk of education.

The girl child education in India should be empowered more. For each and every girl of this nation, who is interested in studying, our great government provides funds and scholarships. India has advanced in terms of high-quality treats, treats, and other types of behavior. The students eat well. Hence India through communication.

Proposal for girl child education in India. According to the statistics, whoever is able to be able will be rich and capable. With time, the Indian education system is undergoing changes. Inspection is done. Learning method and curriculum. Aspects that were considered core can be replaced. There can be a shift in skill development. Skills such as support, communication, empathy, competence, adaptability, and competence. The game has now been played in the game. OK, so contact us. Has been made offline online offline, and a revolutionary change has been made in the world. Integrated and Experimental perspectives are implemented in a single system. Along with being able to communicate systems like environmental, global, feminine communication, communication will also improve.

If we consider this pandemic time, the education system is really affected a lot but we can see many changes in it. The effect is impacting the great at a major level. We can see the factors that have affected the change. The way of learning and the curriculum with other major changes. There will be a major change in consideration for the progress of life skills. We can observe the skills like collaboration, communication, self-resilience, adaptability, empathy, emotional intelligence, and many more. This is amazing and will now be encouraged with empowerment in schools and new purposes, visions will be considered for future. Yes, the learning is going to be the same but new methods might be adopted with digitalization. New education policy will play a great role in national welfare and student empowerment. We can see that education is switched from offline to online, and it is going to be the best example. Yes, it is creating a great revolution in the world. Experiential and practical learning will be implemented in the learning system from the school level. The major problems of nation and world will be focused on the environment, global warming, climate change, women empowerment, casteism, discrimination, etc, towards betterment. The new system will focus on a better future morally and ethically.

Firstly, when a young child learns the three R's in his life, it is the imperative duty of our education system to make learning easy and interesting for him. I think the best way to do this is to teach in the same language in which they were trained to speak in their childhood, that is, to teach in their mother tongue. This will improve the education system by making it less difficult to learn English in a foreign language by reading and writing in the mother tongue.

Secondly, to further analyze the discussion of the medium of instruction i.e. English versus English. Regarding the indigenous language of the country, it is worth mentioning here that there has been an increase in English medium schools in our country in the last two decades. So, it is also true that at the school level, there is a huge trend towards 'English' as a foreign language. Also, I would like to say that English should be welcomed at this level of higher education because in today's globalized world this level of education has a global outlook on higher education. Reducing the pressure of a young child to learn a foreign language is not welcome as it puts immense pressure on him to face the foreign language at a very young age. Third, today's education system is more focused on innovation, knowledge, and creativity than stress. Recently, the eyes of many people in our country were closed on giving grace marks by CBSE. And in the final examinations of class X and XII by the state board in states like Assam. This temporary arrangement to get more and more students to pass the 10th and 12th exams is a complete suicide. So in recent times, many students were able to clear 10th and 12th exams with flying colors but since then their journey of success has come to a halt. In this context, I suggest that our education system should be knowledge-centered rather than focusing more on the academic achievement of the students associated with innovative thinking, creativity, etc. Instead of getting rich by studying a branch of study or subject, the student in your education system should try to enrich that branch of study through basic research and innovation.

I think, right now our teaching method has more emphasis on less study in the life and the general public has earned more or less in life. Chanakya, Kabir, Swami Vivekananda, Dnayaneshwar Mauli, Sant Tukaram Maharaj, Chattrapati Shivaji Maharaj and countless other saints have enriched India with their knowledge of this land in the past, but nowadays most of us are seen studying to join the white-collar rat race. Jobs. So there are many graduates in our country but there are few Steve Jobs or Newtons or Elon Musk or TATA or Ambani and Adani in this country. In this context, we should consider whether we are able to carry on the legacy of the past through our current education system, and if not, we should introspect what has gone wrong. We all Indians need to stand up and start a start-up campaign in our country to remove the current impasse in our education system in support of the new education system with more modifications in the future. One of the biggest goals to make our education system a future fit is to inculcate a sense of moral discipline in combination with what is taught by the teachers and make it morally strong for the students. Values are at a crossroads in Indian society at this time. Therefore the educated public is in a dilemma whether to become a fierce knowledge-seeker or a fierce money-seeker in his life. What I want to tell them in this context is that wealth is worldly but what is divine in life is knowledge. The knowledge that takes us to the path of divinity should be welcomed by all. I think all of us Indians should keep in mind that knowledge is ubiquitous in any education system but the laziness and enthusiasm brought by money are just that.

In short, I would like to say that the most important improvement I want to make in my education system is to make it affordable and accessible to all. In this endeavor, in a developing country like ours, we must focus on its sovereignty, or in other words, on the doorstep of every Indian. I think in this context, all of us Indians, including our policymakers, should strive for universal education in our country as it is universal suffrage in our country. On the contrary, our education system will become a silver-lined and pound fool type concept in our country. If we have to include our nation among the developed countries of the world, then a major change has to be brought into the education system of the country. Because a developed country pays a lot of attention to its education. For this, all of us Indians have to adopt a practical approach in education by not running after degrees. Even the big companies of the world today employ youth with a practical approach without looking at the degree. It also includes big companies like Facebook, Google, and Microsoft. We can also be the change. Let us start producing awareness and create positive vibes with an extra positive environment. You are on a different journey. You have everything you need off. Start and be the change.

E. THE RECENT SCENARIO – YOUTHS MOVING TOWARDS SOCIAL CHANGE AND ROLE IN COMMUNITY.

Youths of the nation play really a great role towards betterment of society and mankind. But don't you think, we should be providing such education, which not only prepares the youth who are job seekers, but also create job-creating students. For this, intensive efforts to promote entrepreneurship will have to be continued continuously. The new coronavirus has caused great destruction in India. Don't you think so? Our Gross Domestic Product (GDP) forecasts have moved towards negative growth rates. The country is being hit hard by unemployment. There is a fear of the reverse momentum of progress towards poverty alleviation. However, the worst effects of this epidemic are seen to be falling on the youth of teenagers and specifically from 21 to 35 age-group the most. Together they are facing many challenges. Along with severe unemployment and disruption in education, they are also facing the brunt of the failing education system. The effort of the government should be that it should not only help the youth to get rid of the current economic crisis but also try to avoid the population crisis that India is facing at this time. To deal with the comparatively worse impact of the pandemic on the youth of India, the government must make special efforts. The effort of the government should be that it should not only help the youth to get rid of the current economic crisis but also try to avoid the population crisis that India is facing at this time. What is your opinion on this? I think the adults experienced minds of the nation can contribute a lot in this scenario.

Due to this Covid-19 pandemic, the education of around seventy percent of the youth all over the world has been hampered. In India, since there is a severe disparity between different communities in terms of the availability of education, then here the education of the youth is seen to be disturbed the most. Young women have been the worst affected by the disruption in studies due to the pandemic. The main reason for this is that they have to work more at home and in return they do not even get money. Evidence from the Ebola crisis tells us that due to the epidemic, girls and young women were more pressured to drop out than boys. The crisis of the pandemic reduces household income and increases the economic challenges, so young boys and girls, especially in rural areas, leave their studies and start working to help their families. Apart from this, another major reason why education is hampered during the pandemic is the huge disparity in the availability of digital resources. There is a lot of inequality in India when it comes to having smartphones. The same situation is also in the case of internet facilities. For this reason, many students of India are facing the challenge of long-term disruption in their education. Although schools have been opened in some areas, yet online education is being promoted more so that the crowd of students does not gather. Digital discrimination, the increased burden of working without pay at home, and the crisis of urgently addressing the challenge of declining household incomes have caused massive disruptions to young people's education. There is a fear of increasing inequality going forward. This is expected to reduce the development of human capital and increase unemployment further.

All the institutional, different education boards of the country and different education systems of different states have also contributed a lot in worsening the very worrying condition of unemployment and education among the youth. Because the education system of every state is dealing with the crisis of this epidemic in its own way, which is having an impact on the students graduating in the coming time. The delay in conducting the examination is also delaying the recruitment of final year students. This has cast a shadow of uncertainty and despair among the youth. Due to this, job opportunities are being completely lost at the hands of many youths. This is not only troublesome in the short term, but it is going to have an impact on employment and wages in the long term as well. The delay in conducting the examination is also delaying the recruitment of final year students. This has cast a shadow of uncertainty and despair among the youth. Due to this, job opportunities are being completely lost at the hands of many youths. This is not only troublesome in the short term, but it is going to have an impact on employment and wages in the long term as well. The reason is that jobs and salaries are not only based on education and skills, but they are also directly related to earlier employment. If one has been unemployed in the period between two jobs, then there is a risk of going down the full growth rate of jobs and salaries. Even before this epidemic of corona, the labour force participation rate among the youth was decreasing rapidly. According to observation and current comparison, in the year 2004-05, where it was 56.4 percent, in 2018-19, the labour force participation rate of youth came down to only 38.1 percent. Even more worrying was the NLET figures. Under NLET i.e. Not in

Labour Force, Education and Training, the number of people who are neither working, nor looking for work, nor have they received any kind of education or training are doing nothing. The past financial and economic crises have made the situation worse. The result of this has been that today the youth of the country is very weak financially and during all the economic challenges, the unemployment rate is highest among the youth. The pandemic Covid-19 virus is no other exception to this. The number of such youth in India is more than ten crores. And this figure is when the government has made many efforts to teach new skills to the idle youth of the country, to promote entrepreneurship among them, and to create employment. The past financial and economic crises have made the situation worse. The result of this has been that today the youth of the country is very weak financially and during all the economic challenges, the unemployment rate is highest among the youth. The pandemic of the Covid-19 virus is really no other exception to this. Evidence indicates that the unemployment rate among youth is more sensitive to the business cycle.

The current economic conditions arising due to the pandemic are no different. During the economic crisis, youth are often more likely to be fired. The reason for this is their lack of skill and experience. The burden of contract working culture in India is also more on the youth. Compared to them, older workers are more likely to get permanent jobs now. Evidence from the Ebola crisis tells us that due to the epidemic, girls and young women were more pressured to drop out than boys. The crisis of the pandemic reduces household income and increases the economic challenges, so young boys and girls, especially in rural areas, leave their studies and start working to help their families. Due to contract work, the employment situation of the youth becomes very delicate. According to a study conducted by the International Labour Organization, the unemployment rate among youth was found to be three times higher than before the epidemic of Covid-19, and the coronavirus epidemic has only worsened the situation. There are many challenges before the youth of today's world. Today the youth of India is facing a trio of challenges. They are facing unemployment due to poor job market conditions, the disruption in the education system has increased the pressure to drop out and the youth of the country are also facing difficulties due to the digital gap. Due to continuous delays in the examination, they are neither getting degrees nor are they free to look for jobs. Now time is running out of India's hands and the country is rapidly moving towards becoming a nation of the elderly. In such a situation, there is a need to take quick steps so that the country can stop its biggest asset – the youth of the country from becoming a burden. The pandemic of COVID-19 has not only adversely affected the economic and physical health of the country, but has also deprived it of reaping the benefits of the power of its youth. Now time is running out of India's hands and the country is rapidly moving towards becoming a nation of the elderly. In such a situation, there is a need to take quick steps so that the country can stop its biggest asset – the youth of the country from becoming a burden. The sectors that have seen maximum employment generation in the last decade are manufacturing, construction, trade, hotels, and transport. Due to this epidemic, the worst effect has been seen on these sectors of the economy. In order to rejuvenate these sectors, there is a need for massive government investment and concerted efforts especially with the aim of helping the young population. I think special efforts will also have to be made for this so that there is the least obstacle in continuing education and the gap in the availability of digital resources can be reduced between different communities of youth.

According to a recent survey conducted by the National Sample Survey Office of the Government of India, today less than a quarter of the households in the country have internet access. To save the youth from the ravages of unemployment, there is a need to introduce many programs reforming our nation towards Youth Reformation. In this, it is very necessary to arrange respectable work to give more emphasis on giving employment to the youth. The number of such households with the internet is less than ten percent where students live. Not all states, but the governments of many states have taken such steps so that the problem of students dropping out can be minimized. This requires a larger and comprehensive approach, isn't it?

At the same time, there is a need for the intervention of the central government in this matter, every state has its own capacity to deal with these challenges. In such a situation, due to the absence of a uniform effort run by the centre across the country, inequality will start developing at the regional level among the youth. In addition, the emphasis should be on imparting such education, which not only prepares the youth for job seekers but also creates job-creating students. For this, intensive efforts to promote entrepreneurship will have to be continued continuously. The concerted effort of the industrial community and the government should continue to create a well-functioning skills demand-supply system. There can also be different approaches to deal with such problems. As youths are moving towards social change and they play a very vital role in the community. I think the retired people known as adults can help out. It is so simple, to my dear adults of the nation – you are retired but you are still young by mindset. You have a great experience, you know about mistakes, you can be the creators of new and extra-skilled youths of the nation. If you take a resolution that you will train at least 5 budding youths of the nation around you, can really make a difference on large scale. Think about it, you can do that. Young people reading this can approach such expertise individuals and can really contribute greatly towards the nation.

F. TRUE EMPOWERMENT-YOUTHS ARE FOR LEADERSHIP.

If we consider the social and political scenario of the country from past to the present time, we can easily guess that India has a very strong need for leadership and need Empowered youth power. The current Leader, Sir PM Narendra Modi Ji is the very best example of leadership. We need the right direction to emerge in India by taking out the politics of accusations, fasting, and agitations, which should provide an opportunity to the people to cooperate in the development of the country by taking decisions in the public interest. And for all this, we have to get rid of this mentality that "today's politics is the last refuge of filthy and thieves and dacoits". Don't you think this is very important? How long will we keep pushing the common people into the deep abyss of inflation and corruption by making all these excuses? If politics is dirty then whose responsibility is it to clean it? Are we not responsible for the same? Today the public is in search of such a young leader, who understands that the hopes of 136.6 crore people are attached behind it. To get rid of the terrorists who have the support of 19 crore people, do not forget the power of 136.6 crore people while spreading their hands in front of the government which has the support of fewer people in the ratio of the public. Is it not our duty to start the change? But for this, we have to recognize the intention of those people who, for their selfishness, push the confident youth power into the fast-moving and the politics of the prisoners.

Even today, the guidance of the world is possible only through Indian philosophy, but this heritage of ours has again been noticed by others in the whole world, and we have to protect this heritage of ours. Don't you think about it as the youth of the nation? If you, take some successful actions. We should know that we are the children of Chanakya who can train a boy playing in the mud and make him a Chakravarti emperor like Chandragupta Maurya. The Maurya dynasty produced a ruler like Emperor Ashoka, during which time the Maurya Empire extended from the ranges of the Hindukush in the north to the south of the Godavari River and Mysore in the south, and from Bengal in the east to Afghanistan in the west. Whereas today others in the world are making their claim on our own land, and our leadership is watching the spectacle silently. Today India is the youngest country in the world, isn't it?. India is the only country in the world where around an estimated 64% and more of the people are in the age group of 15-64 and youngsters. This is the power we have and also this is the opportunity we have as youngsters. Human resource is the biggest and fastest paying resource of any country. But in India, this resource is being sacrificed for the politics of votes. What I mean is that we light a lamp in our house before lighting the world. And for this, there is a need for strong leadership who does not get distracted by the horses from across the border and creates such possibilities in our own country that our young generation can become a flame of its own extinguished lamp.

Dear reader consider it in practical form, we talk on many perspectives that we have to change politics like this and like that, But don't you think we are only thinking of it? We have to do something new in it. That means every youth thinks about bringing change by just talking on stage, protest or talking on katts - with friends. Whereas to bring back the lost leadership in students in every sector along with politics, we have to do a lot. We just cant keep talking. We need to develop new ideas, new visions, and much more innovative approaches. Don't you think it is required for today? Leadership is a very important factor and you can develop it automatically if you decide it. Every person in our country has the thought of removing the dirt without spoiling his hands. How is it possible? To remove the filth of politics, the youth will have to spoil their hands. If united you can change the scenario. Why youths are getting distracted? Wake up, you have to achieve a lot. The inner soul gets totally disappointed when I observe the youths around me and all over the nation sometimes talking about politics, political decisions, smoking, drinking, flirting, or talking major but useless talks. I get disappointed because these people don't even know the preamble printed on the very first page of every academic textbook but then also the distracted youth keep judging the decisions by the government. It is so bad on our path, isn't it? I am not saying don't talk about politics, but I am saying talk with proper study and develop your intellectual personality. It is very important and for sure it will take our nation towards extra boosted progress in analogy. This is the time where your leadership can be proved. One of the major reasons for losing student leadership is that we change our thinking under someone's pressure, then it may be college management or family. If we have the ability of student leadership then every youth should come under any pressure and do their work better. Only then the number of young entrepreneurs, young successful people, quality engineers, quality agriculturists, quality reformers, and intellectual thinkers, activists, and youth politicians in our politics will increase. Just as we get jobs by giving interviews in campus placements, in the same way, politicians should be admitted only after giving interviews to build clean politics. This will impact a lot, isn't it? Because intellectual mindsets will sit on the chair of parliament house of Central and states development. The youth of the country certainly has leadership potential, but due to the politics of selfishness, student leadership is not getting better opportunities.

Youths have to wake up and start doing innovative things in it. After all, youths are the ultimate source of power and storehouse of innovative ideas and visions. Party politics is also misleading the youth leadership. To improve the position of student leadership, we can also have a leader of students who are selected on the basis of merit proper abilities, intellectual personality, and capability but not supporting discrimination of caste, colour, or any other selfish thoughts. Also, he should have the ability to solve all the problems of the students and people at ground level. Only then we young students can build a bright future in politics with proper leadership. Every human being has leadership potential and youths are at the front here. But before doing any work, we look more towards the negative aspects of it. Just like we do not want to come into politics by seeing nepotism in politics, but if we young people come into politics with a positive mindset, then maybe we can also make a change through better leadership. The youth in the present generation are trying to take on leadership roles that were earlier reserved for the seniors, a move that has not been received by the elders in the most positive form of light. Despite all the struggles, youth are encouraged to join leadership positions to represent their demographic, but also to ensure that they develop themselves into great future leaders.

The experience is a very important part of one's leadership journey. I advise you all dear readers, you young people to take this as an opportunity to learn and gain practical experience with your practice for increasing leadership quality. Also, youth-led organizations should create a good and welcoming environment for the youth to volunteer and practice their leadership journey. There are many things by which we can improve our leadership quality, Participate in student government, Join or start a club, get involved in sports teams or other after-school activities, Find volunteering opportunities, Get an internship, Complete a passion project along with its focus on qualities such as being goal-oriented, being honest, being hardworking, Willing to serve others, being good listener, being good communicator, being good decision-maker, Encouraging, being Positive, Responsible and much more as required.

G. YOUTH AND TECHNOLOGY.

Youths - Technology, The term technology is related to science. Technology is a science that deals with problem-solving or inventing useful tools which help humans to do their work more efficiently. Nowadays! Technology is developed everywhere in every field including education and farming. Technology makes human life easier and comfortable. We can access any information within the world simply by using World Wide Web abbreviated as www from the comfort of our home. Technology gives us the power to travel within the world with the help of airplanes, ships which saves our lot of time. In past, peoples are unaware of what was happening in their society and the country due to the lack of technology, although there were newspapers that take a lot of time including manufacturing and all to reach their readers. Now with the help of technology, it becomes very easy for us to know what is happening anywhere in the world. Television technology gives us all that information very rapidly. Apart from this, one of the best technology, the smartphone is a great boon for the people living in this modern era. The smartphone is a great technology which gives us great flexibility, it comes with all the things including search engine, camera, even we can see new and movies in it just like we see in our to. It is the combination of all the features which are very essential in today's life.

Nowadays it also replaces pen and paper, people write their ideas, articles, or any important thing on their smartphones in soft copy format with the help of a note app which is available on every smartphone. They are light in weight, handy, and easy to carry. Smartphone saves our lot of time and gives us great comfortability to do our work anywhere. Because of technology research is simplified. There are a lot of simulation software available in every field from vehicle manufacturing to PCB designing which helps us to first try our idea in that, if it successfully works, then implement it in the real world. This simulation technology saves a lot of time as well as a lot of money by simply giving us results before implementing them practically. Technology gives us luxurious life by adding so many devices like fans, AC, cars in our life which give us great comfort, apart from any weather conditions. So technology is a great boon for us if we used it in the appropriate manner. Otherwise, this technology has the power to develop nations as well as the power to destroy the nations. Technology has been the primary source of military innovation thought history. It helps and also pace in warfare changes more than any other factor. Airplanes, missiles, tanks, drones, satellites, computers, GPS, these all are used in military operations which leads to a lot of destruction, including people's life. Similarly, technology has the power to change the life of youths in a proper manner that can benefit them, as well as in an inappropriate manner that destroys them. We know that eating is a basic necessity of life, but we don't eat continuously, we know that if we eat in a proper manner it will benefit us but if we overeat it will harm us. Most of the youths use technology only for enjoying the comfort of it. Because of this, such a great boon becomes a curse for them. They use smartphones only for using social media, for useless talking. Seeing and doing inappropriate things which consume their lot of important time which directly affect their studies. With the help of technology, youths can study a lot of new things from the top professors from all around the world and can achieve anything in their life. But somehow, a lot of youths are learning inappropriate things. Excessive use of smartphones leads to health issues among many youths. Youths are totally living in the digital world which results in low contact with the real world.

There is a lot of difference between the real world and the digital world, when they can't match with the real world they become frustrated and somehow they start overthinking. Technology makes human life easy and comfortable but it makes youths lazy, they are not able to do anything without using technology. They forgot their real powers and they are totally dependent on technology. Technology includes video games in the life of youths because of which they are only playing virtually not physically. That majorly affects physical as well as mental health.

From this, we conclude that we can't use technology? No. Technology is really a great boon for us it is our responsibility to use it with care and for the benefit of other people as well as for our benefit. If youths learned that how to use this great weapon, then definitely it will change their lives in a positive manner and they can do anything great in this world.

49

H. YOUTHS AND DISTRACTIONS – CAN YOU SKIP UNWANTED RELATIONSHIPS BY FOLLOWING RESPONSIBILITIES.

We are young people and yes each and every person of us has some responsibility towards society, family, friends and his work. We have to be serious to do this, isn't it? We should work hard to fulfill our responsibility. In all these obligations, it is our main responsibility to do something towards the country. We must fulfill it in some way or the other. We should always come forward to help the needy, raise our voice against corruption. By making the younger generation cultured, by making them understand well and bad, we can also build a good society. Today's youth is forgetting to respect their values, morals, and ethics in the overconfidence of the modern world towards elders. I want to be a successful and responsible citizen in my life. I want to modernize my society by fulfilling my obligations towards society and the country. In the society in which we live, it is necessary for every person to have a house to live in, three meals a day to eat, clothes, and things for convenience. As citizens of the country, we should help the needy. I want every person in society to be educated and intelligent. It is also our responsibility to provide education to those who are not able to read. Everything is correct but is it really possible. Yes, my dear friends if we avoid all the distractions taking us towards devils place then everything is possible. Youths of the nation are the main and beautiful artwork of God in the world and man is a social animal. As youths, we are bound by certain human sensitivities, needs, expectations, and beliefs, which are directly related to our personal, social, family, and national life without any legal, classical, religious, or caste restrictions. Their sustenance is the main under our moral obligation. Without the desire for any profit, selfishness, or reward, it also comes in our responsibility to contribute to the good wishes of others, public welfare, and everyone's interest.

Rather than getting distracted by girlfriends, boyfriends, or porn. My young people, you are a unique creation on this earth. So stay calm and work for betterment. Let us make a unique confluence of the method of making today's young generation future and character and being attested by mythological knowledge, modern technology and science will take the future of our self and youths towards a golden path. If everyone becomes good then surely the whole society will also become good. The main aim of education as a youth of this nation is to make the disciples decent and educated and not only literate. As the youths of this nation, it becomes our responsibility to inculcate moral values in the distracted public and interact with them daily about the values. If there is talk of youth empowerment and reformation daily, with our great old personalities like Gautama Buddha, Swami Vivekananda, Dr.APJ kalam sir, etc through seminars, awareness programs, books, competitions, and much more activities, then all the distracted public of the nation themselves will be aware of the moral values and values, due to which our responsibility will also be fulfilled. Every responsible person in the world should fulfill his responsibilities diligently. Everyone's goal is different. Some wanted to become a doctor and some wanted to be an engineer, but mine and people like you reading this book should have different aims simultaneously. By making the youths of the nation aware of the importance of education, they can create interest in education in them. It is our responsibility to be aware of the new consciousness, new awakening, and our rights in society. Being conscious of one's duty, one should never lag behind in fulfilling one's own obligations towards society. To sensitize this generation moving towards darkness, every person has to fulfill the responsibility that he should show the right path to the new generation. This should be the responsibility of all of our lives. All the people living in the society should be motivated from time to time towards their responsibilities. There may be some beings who have nothing to do with responsibilities. It is your responsibility to fulfill your responsibilities properly. As a youth of this nation, I want to say that today's distracted do not have the patience that they used to have in ancient times. Remove the bad qualities in them and fill in the good qualities. The distracted public should be taught morality, etiquette, good thoughts, respect, humility, and tolerance. They should be taught ancient texts so that they can understand how elders should be treated and what our social, worldly, and national responsibilities are. In the Modern world, the question has become strong that whether every person in society is fulfilling his responsibilities or not. If yes, why is there an atmosphere of dissatisfaction spreading in society? Why are youths getting distracted and addicted? This picture of the society is intimidating, in which youths of the nation are being murdered by the distracted public. So someone is committing atrocities on their parents, who created them and enabled them. Somewhere the incidents of humiliation, theft, robbery, exploitation, drug abuse, corruption of women are confusing the coming generation. In this, it becomes our responsibility to create awareness, moral lessons to this wandering generation, so that they can get the values. If you have good values, you will also be able to know the difference between good and bad. Swami Vivekananda ji has said that by recognizing the infinite power and power of the mind, a person can not only become thoughtful but can also convert into a good person. If the foundation of the house is weak then there is a danger of the house getting destroyed. If a human does not have the responsibility towards humanity and culture and society, then his life is helpless and useless. Human beings can become human only through humanity.

As a youth of this nation, it becomes our responsibility that we impart knowledge about the culture and society to the distracted public. It is our responsibility to build future citizens for the society and the nation by doing all-round development of children. Together we all should inculcate values in this distracted public. When every citizen of the nation will leave the feeling of selfishness and keep the feeling of patriotism, then he will be able to recognize his responsibilities. We should be mindful of our responsibilities. As a part of society, we should fulfill the responsibility of eradicating the evils spread in society. Understanding my responsibility, I will try to curb corruption. Corruption has hollowed out our country. I consider it my responsibility to get strict punishment for the corrupt, bribe-takers, and oppressors. Along with this, it is my responsibility to respect my parents, gurus, and elders and also have affection for the younger ones. Can you do it? Try once and it is the best satisfaction you will experience. God has given man the power to think and understand differently.

If we leave the values and morals and start becoming cultureless, then what will be the difference between man and animal? It is our responsibility to motivate the stray to walk on the good path with good conduct and affection and kindness. As the youth of this nation, don't you think this is correct? Before fulfilling my dreams, it is my duty to do whatever I can for the country. As a youth of this nation just think once. Is it not your responsibility and duty to contribute? Then decide it you're your way, dear reader. I want to do something for the country. Like removing poverty, helping the helpless people, and ensuring the safety of women in the country, I consider it my responsibility. Before all these things, I want to change the thinking of the people of the country. If we change our thinking, our country will automatically change. It should be our responsibility to put in the distracted public the feeling of true love for the country from the very beginning.

I. YOUTHS AND SOCIAL MEDIA.

Very first of all we should know, what is social media? Social media is a computer technology that allows us to share our ideas, information, and thoughts with other people. Let us see the most common examples of social media from our day-to-day life which are Instagram, Facebook, youtube, and many more. Social media plays a very important role in faster communication and yes that is really great. With the help of social media, one can easily communicate with each other without any obstacles and from anywhere within the world which saves a lot of time. Because of social media, we get in touch with our friends all the time apart from any condition whether we are present in the same place or not. Social media is greatly beneficial for educational purposes to obtain useful information. If we want to learn a particular subject for that there is a lot of material available on social media which helps us a lot. With the help of social media, we can learn any art including singing, dancing, music, instrument learning from the comfort of our home. For this YouTube is the best example so there are a lot of chances of increasing the skills of a person. But somewhere are we addicted to it? Not a single minute of today's youth is going without electronic devices. Is it not harming our mental health? Also, Social media is a source of income for many people and it is heaven for the people of social media marketing. Social media is a great medium, a great opportunity for many peoples who are talented in their particular fields and wants to present their talent in front of others. Nowadays social media is also used for shopping which saves our time and gives us great comfort. So from that, we know that there are a lot of advantages of social media, but everything has two faces one is good and one is bad. Although social media can present some risks, it is important to understand what benefits our youth needs to follow the guidelines they need to make the best out of their social media use.

Below is a list of ways social media can be a good resource for youths can learn and appreciate different perspectives and worldviews to better understand the world around them and build their knowledge on various topics. With so many ideas shared across multiple platforms, they can discover areas of interest and use the platforms in an educational capacity. As social media is now a neighbourhood of lifestyle, it's important for youngsters and to find out the way to communicate online to organize them for future opportunities in the workplace and to support them in interactions with friends and family. Social media removes the limits of meeting and maintaining people and building bonds beyond boundaries. For youths of our nation who may have a disability or don't feel like they can connect with others within their community, this can be a great way to share ideas and interests connecting many youths and every other personality. Access to family members who may live miles apart from friends who have moved from a local area can maintain relationships and allow them to stay in touch and share their lives with ease. This can open up opportunities to supply support to friends and family who could also be experiencing a specific issue. On the flip side for a few youths, this will be an area where they will seek support if they're browsing something they cannot ask about it.

They can help, raise awareness of the particular cause they want to make an impact on the real world to effect change where they want to see it. Young people use their accounts to share their achievements, showcase their talents, and can also share to CVs to build a positive online portfolio to benefit them later in life. Social media is really very great power, a great weapon for youths to change themselves for their well-being.

But great power comes with great responsibility. Social media is good if youths used it in the right way otherwise, it becomes a great distraction for youths. Most of the youths are unaware of how to use social media, they used social media only for their entertainment purposes which lead to distraction. It is also the responsibility of parents to check whether their children required smartphones or not from which they use social media. Are they mature enough to use them? Due to lack of proper guidance, youths are using social media in the wrong way, they think social media is just to show how rich we are, how to look smarter and cooler, how to attract people from another gender, and just to fulfil their lusty thoughts. Slowly youths are getting attracted to it. Youths are connected with each other only within social media and not physically which leads to a lack of emotional connection, they become lazy which adversely affects their health. Physical interactions are very important for humans, it is their basic nature and here because youths are not physically connected their face to face communication skill gets reduced which results in a decrease in their self -confidence. On social media we don't know another person accurately that he is good or not, he is well-mannered or not, just by seeing someone's photo, how can we identify their character? This is the main reason because of which many peoples face cyberbullying.

Social media also comes with the glamour of materialist things where people show their glamorous and luxurious lifestyle which includes costly things like cars, bungalows, etc. Most of the youths get attracted towards it and they think only this is life and without such things, our life will be bad and useless, and they think this is their ultimate reality which leads to frustration. They think that they are a commodity. Due to excessive use of social media, youths are present everywhere, they are with their parents in a family picnic, and anywhere, but at all the places they are present physically not mentally their mind is in the world of social media which is an artificial world. Youths are lacking understanding and thoughtfulness they are facing a lack of family quality time. Most of the youths compare their life with other people and they compete with each other to fulfill their false materialistic egos. Safety is somewhat affected because of the honey trapping concept in trend. Many girls are trapped and blackmailed for the illegal cause. This is very wrong and we all need to be aware of all these factors.

Unknowingly youths are controlled by social media, everything on social media what we see, what we hear, is controlled by that one app with the help of artificial intelligence, machine learning, data science, and a lot more. Youths are becoming the slave of social media, don't be the slave of social media you have the power to control it, but this is only possible if you control yourself. Self-control is very necessary. Balance is very important in everything. Even in cooking food, if all the things are in proper balance then it becomes delicious, tasty and healthy but if one thing imbalances it tastes different, sometimes not very good. Similarly, this is the relationship between youth and social media which totally depends on the balance of use. If youths use social media very accurately and with proper control it will definitely benefit them and they can do, they can learn anything they want With the help of this great weapon name social media they can achieve great heights of success.

END OF
THE ROAD

J. YOUTHS AND ADDICTION

What is addiction? We hear many times he is addicted, maybe drug-addicted or alcohol-addicted, etc. Commonly we use the word habit for children's, that he has a habit of eating chocolate, here we don't use the word addiction that the child was chocolate addict, No, because addiction is different from the habit. Addiction is more powerful than habit. Addiction is defined as not having control of what we are doing or using something to the point where it could be harmful to us. As we know that it is commonly associated with alcohol, drugs, smoking, etc. A large number of youths are considering these things normal as a part of life and they think this is cool, we are teenagers and without doing such things we lost our precious teenage life. But they don't know because of such habits they unknowingly lost their precious teenage life. Once they get indulged in such habits they get changed, their habits change, their whole personality changes, and at last, they lost their original personality and become addicted personality. Long-term exposure to alcohol leads to the shrinking of the brain. Alcohol can their typical behaviour's and leave them without mental clarity, because of which they are not able to make smart decisions.

Nowadays smoking is very common in every college, it is considered a sign of coolness among teenagers, but they don't know it is a sign of death in the future. Also, there are lots of addictive products which are available on a large scale which includes drugs, charas, tobacco products and lot more which are very very harmful to our health. All of the products are available on a large scale because there is a lot of demand for such things among the youths. There are lots of youths who even lost their beautiful life only by indulging in such addictions. Most of the youths are destroying their careers, their lives, and a lot more. These all the things are really very addictive and very dangerous for our self as well as for others, including our family members. For example, if a person is drunk and he drives a vehicle then that person is very dangerous for other persons which are walking on the road, as he lost his control over it, a major accident can happen. So it becomes very important for us to remain addiction free in our teenage life as well as for whole life if you really want to live your life happily. Is it totally the fault of students that they are indulged and get addicted to such a habit? Really the answer is no. Its human's tendency to learn new things from their association. From our childhood, we learned lots of things from our association, by copying our mother, father, sister, brother, and sometimes neighbours. If we are coming from a good association then definitely we become a good person but if our association is not good we can't say that we become good or not. The association plays a very important role in previous years of learning. When we freshly entered our college we come with a lot of good habits but slowly our habit changes, our behaviour changes, we become a different personality because of our association. Here in that association, we see that everyone including our friends and seniors is talking about smoking and drinking, not only talking but doing in front of us.

By seeing all such things we think that this is common and enjoyable and from here, youths start indulging in such addictions which can definitely destroy them in long term. They don't see what are the disadvantages of such habits that they can cause lung cancer, they only see temporary enjoyment and fake glamour and they jump into the world of addictions We are the youths it is our responsibility to don't promote such things, it is our responsibility that in our association no one gets to indulge in such addictions. It is our responsibility to take care of our self as well as of others. It is not impossible to remove from addictions, just self-realization is necessary, mindset is necessary and most importantly our self-control is necessary.

K. YOUTHS AND POLITICS – A NOVAL TRANSFORMATION.

Youth are an important link in any country's society. Therefore, youth should help people by coming forward in the work of politics, social service, so that together we can build a strong society without discrimination. If human resource is converted into human capital by investing in education, health, and skill development, then it will surely get better returns in future. If human resource is not properly exploited and managed, then it also creates the biggest obstacle in development. What do you think about this? Youth are the main caption of the ship of change in any country and society. History witnesses that all the revolutionary changes that have taken place in the world till date, whether they have been social, political, economic, cultural, and scientific, their main base has been youth. Youths are the ultimate power no doubt. India also has a rich history of youth. In ancient times, from Adiguru Shankaracharya to Gautam Buddha and Mahavir Swami took the initiative of religious and social reform in their youth. In the Renaissance period of our history, young thinkers like Swami Vivekananda along with Raja Rammohun Roy, Swami Dayanand Saraswati led the religious and social reform movement. Swami Vivekananda had hoisted the victory flag of Indian religious philosophy on the strength of his eloquent speech style and scholarship in the Chicago Religion Conference in 1893. After his scintillating speech, the people of western imperialist countries were also taken aback by the Indian knowledge tradition. In modern times, young revolutionaries like Chattrapati Shivaji Maharaj, Chattrapati Sambhaji Maharaj, Saint Dnyaneshwar Mauli, Saint Tukaram Maharaj, Tipu Sultan, Rani Laxmibai, Bhagat Singh, Chandrashekhar Azad, and Netaji Subhash Chandra Bose, Babasaheb Ambedkar had soured the teeth of the British.

Many young leaders have also contributed to making the movements of the Father of the Nation, Mahatma Gandhi was successful and getting India independence under his leadership. If we talk about the history of contemporary India from independence till now, then many movements and changes that took place in this period have been led by the youth. From making India self-reliant in food production (Green Revolution) to nuclear power, the young shoulders took up the responsibility. The computer revolution and new economic policy were also the product of the young mind. Only the youth population can give impetus to the progress of the country. The former President of India Dr. A.P.J. Abdul Kalam had said that I remember is we have immense wealth in the form of youth resources and if this section of the society is empowered then we can achieve the goal of becoming a superpower very soon. In the field of science and technology, the youth of India is ringing in the whole world, but due to talent migration, we are not able to take advantage of them. We have to understand that the progress of the youth will lead to the country. The day the participation of youth will increase from politics to administration, from society to science, from sports to business, the future of the country will shine and it can be the biggest achievement. There is a need for Change and it is going to start with you. Are you ready? If human resource is converted into human capital by investing in education, health, and skill development, then it will surely get better returns in future.

I think it is really unpredictable which way we will go from where we are standing today. The number of youth in the age group of 18 to 35 years is very high in the country. Some are considering it as a national resource. If these youths get the right direction, then they are resources, otherwise, this population full of resentment and annoyance can become trouble for the policy-makers of the country. That's why there is a little fear about the time to come. The youth do not have employment. Do not have a good education. There is no role model. They don't see any hope. A party wants to crown its crown prince as the Prime Minister, but he is not ready for this chair. The question is, if he is not ready, why not leave the field. Why not give someone else a chance? The responsibility of handling the country should be given to the person who has the stamina, the zeal, the passion. On the other hand, there is a leader who wants to occupy the throne of Delhi with the help of politics of hate. He is busy preparing to cash in on the anger of these youths. In these circumstances, it seems that the country is at a dangerous juncture. To be honest, such intolerance has rarely been seen before. Today, if you write something on Facebook against a leader, then a whole gang surrounds you. He can also get abusive with you. In fact, it is also anger against the existing regime and also the support of those who go to any extent to capitalize on that anger.

Our real problem is the absence of a middle class in politics. Talking about Britain and other western countries, the situation is different there. There the middle-class people came into politics, so they changed a lot. Take Margaret Thatcher, her father ran a grocery store. We have middle-class people coming out in every field except politics. In the name of democracy, the dynasty has made a place in politics. Most of the upper-class people are active in politics. The rest of the place has been taken by mafia and criminals. Only then decisions are not taken in our country keeping in mind the long term. Politicians barely think about five years. Today the corporate world is increasing its penetration everywhere. In the name of Corporate Social Responsibility, they are forming NGOs. They are infiltrating our development plans. In this way, their eyes are on our natural resources. They are influencing our policies in this way. Whereas the business of the corporate should have basically been confined to making profits and distributing it among its shareholders. In fact, democracy in our country is continuously weakening. Today, when the Supreme Court reprimands the government on something, the common man is very happy. He looks at the top court with hope. This trend is dangerous for democracy. Those who vent their anger on Facebook and Twitter should also face the fact that in a country with a population of 1,366 million, only 80 million people are on Facebook. Only two crore people have Twitter accounts. Only around 2 or more than two percent of the total rural population of the country is connected to the Internet. After all the ratio is increased nowadays in covid time and digitalization. But it is needless to mention how many hours electricity lasts in rural areas. Coal crises have arrived but no alternative? In such a situation, there is no use fighting a war only on Facebook and Twitter, and Social media. Now the time has come for our youth to come out of the virtual world to the real world and also join politics. Only then will there be hope for change and freedom will also be available from this despair. If human resource is not properly exploited and managed, then it also creates the biggest obstacle in development. For example, we can take youth involved in terrorism, Naxalism, and extremism. Negative elements like terrorism, Naxalism, and extremism also make youth their medium to carry out their designs. For terrorism, the example of Jammu and Kashmir can be taken, where the terrorists have been carrying out their nefarious designs by tricking the youth. In such a difficult situation, the youth are in extra need of proper guidance. India's youth power needs to be used in positive works. There is a need for such sources of inspiration and guides, who can show a positive and better path to the young generation. As far as the field of research and research is concerned, its condition is also not good. It is not that there is a dearth of talent in the country. When the youth of the country go to countries like America, Britain, France, they get their talents recognized there and also get prestigious prizes. It is 100% true that a country can develop without mineral resources, but without human resources, the development of the country cannot even be thought of. People consider unemployment as one of the reasons for the misguided youth and going on the wrong path. But the youth have to change their mindset that government job is the only way of employment. It is a common belief in Indian society that a government job is the measure of success in life. The people of the society have to change this perception. There is no dearth of opportunities for employment and self-employment in the modern era of liberalization and information revolution. India is the largest democratic country in the world. Despite this, the participation of youth in politics is very less here. It has often been seen that there is a sense of negativity in the youth about politics, so they do not want to come into politics. But they should understand that unless they participate in politics, negativity will not go away from politics. The Indian Constitution has given the right to vote to the youth above the age of eighteen years. In such and every situation the role of youth becomes very important.

While it would be unrealistic and one-sided to expect perfection in an ethically flawed environment in politics, on the other hand, it cannot be denied that the norms set in politics have a significant impact on other aspects of governance. The criminalization of politics - 'the participation of criminals in the election process - has become a delicate part of our electoral system. There are many root causes for the increase in crime and violence to the point of inciting the 'mafia' in many areas of society. Ignorance of laws, poor quality of services and existing corruption, protection of lawbreakers on the basis of political, class, category, sect, or caste, partisan interference in the investigation of crimes, slow prosecution of cases, extraordinary delay of years in the judicial process And the high cost, the indiscriminate grant of parole, the withdrawal of numerous cases, etc. are the reasons that are more important. Expenditure of a large number of illegal and unfair money in elections is another root cause of corruption. Although there is a formal limit on election expenditure and some steps have been taken to curb it, yet in reality, this expenditure is alleged to be excessive. Cleanly conducted elections are a very important way to inculcate moral values in politics, prevent corruption and organize the administration properly. The positive start can only be given by Youths of the nation, so I will say the youngsters of the nation, Wake up and Start getting Aware about such things. Let your Actions speak.

Eating chocolates or popping pills
won't reduce depression.Instead,
one must read Gita. This will help
relieve the stress and depression in
life. It will help in dealing with
challenges of life.
— Sushma Swaraj —

L. New era youth towards Meditation, spirituality, and Mental health.

What is meditation? Is it really helpful to us? Mediation is not about, that you became a very different personality within the time span of one day. Meditation is what gives you deep rest. Meditation is a process in which the seeker sits and loses the mind. "Meditation is not concentration, it is the opposite of concentration," Meditation begins when the mind is free from restlessness and calm and stable. To become a good student requires a lot of time that you study regularly. Practice regularly and revise regularly. After doing all these steps one can say that he is a good student. To maintain our physical health to go with the trend to maintain the body, we go to the gym it helps us to fight the various diseases and makes us fit. But to maintain our mind and to know our inner soul and ourselves we don't have gyms so, here meditation plays a very important role. It is an exercise for the mind. Meditation is the practice of deeply focusing our minds. That also promotes relaxation, mindfulness, and a better sense of inner peace.

Meditation is very important in life. The normal lifestyle of man acquires new vision through meditation. In this view, the personal analysis of the prejudices of life provides intellectual freedom to the person to think and understand. Meditation does not mean the constant recollection of any physical, worldly, and elusive thought or feeling with the eyes closed. While being physically present in worldly activities, if the focus of the individual feeling stimulates the non-worldly being, then it should be understood that life rests on meditation. Meditation also does not mean being fixed towards elusive attractions like wealth, position, and fame. Meditation empowers a person to conduct invocations throughout life, which leads to the quenching of disorders. The seriousness and serious stillness of meditation create positive situations around a person. It gives freedom from the bonds of anger, lust, greed, and attachment. Controlling negative emotions is practiced by staying meditative. It is very meaningful to get victory over the deviation of personality by this method. In this process, the help of society, government, business, and relations are not required. This is a valuable way to become self-realized for oneself. Even after failing in material work, wishing for new success in the subconscious mind and staying away from the negative reactions of the outside world on failures is possible only through meditation. We can carefully put our personality in many public welfare works. For example, the practitioner can use the personal qualities gained from the practice of meditation to make the patient healthy. Similarly, people doing different enterprises in the world can carefully orient their acquired personal utilities and make them people-oriented. Meditation is a simple way to get rid of the misconceptions and illusions of the mind and subconscious mind.

Meditation should be spiritual expansion. With its help, the attraction of objects is destroyed and an unshakable determination to be free from obstacles and vices is formed. What is the goal of human life, proper answers to this question can definitely be found by the daily practice of meditation.

God has especially given the mind, intellect, and soul to man. Through these, he can be discreet and connect the soul with society and the soul with the divine. Apart from the physical body and the senses, God has given a person such a form that he can live by establishing a balance with all. Only then can he make his life successful. A human character can be divided into three parts. First, there are God-given qualities and defects. The development of those characteristics is on the basis of heredity. In the second part, the behaviour of parents, brothers, and sisters also affects the character of the child. In the third part, the school environment, teacher and students as well as the child's neighbourhood, social living, behaviour, and environment also occupy a special place in influencing the character more. The character of the third part can be termed as an acquired character. In the present time, the root cause of increasing immoral activities in the world is the aimless education provided by these three institutions of character building. In short words I will say, we are always inspired and advised by spirituality to take the name god. It may be of any cast, religion, and anything. Don't you think taking the same name in the repeated manner with the same pace, same tone and same word in short chanting is a part of meditation? Yes, it is a part of meditation. Parents, teachers, and senior and enlightened people and saints of the society should consider the deteriorating level of human character. Adults and older people should influence infants, adolescents, and youth through their behaviour and conduct to create an inspiring environment of high character standards. If we all improve our conduct and become good characters and children imitate our behaviour, then crimes can automatically end. Children must be given spiritual education imbued with the inspiration of devotion to God. In today's glare, man is becoming very attached to wealth and pleasures. Mahatma Gandhi had said that true education is that which can make the character of human body, mind, and soul by all-round development.

Is there any way to remain good in a bad association? Yes. This is possible only if we are doing the right things including meditation. Meditation gives us the power to control our mind which helps us to stay far from bad habits. Because of certain addictions and excessive use of social media youths are suffering from Frustration, anxiety, and depression. Meditation definitely helps youths to overcome such situations. Also, spirituality is very important to build a student's character. Character plays a very important role in every aspect of life. A good character person takes the right decision at the right place and time. If we want to control our mind, so, first of all, it is necessary we control our lifestyle. A lot of youths have no proper schedule, they don't have a proper routine. They are continuously wasting their precious time by using social media at night time, which affects their sleep cycle which leads to anxiety. One should must follow Vedic routine to improve their Lifestyle. Vedic routine is very simple just wake up early before sunrise and sleep early after sunset. Eat simple food and stay simple. If youths started doing meditation and just follow a small amount of spirituality then they can easily change this bad environment by their good efforts.

The increasing percentage of youths ending their life and news makes me write about SUICIDE? Why do you feel suicidal? The feeling of being separated from that person on the death of a very close one. If there is any problem in your relationship, In the event of any kind of misbehaviour, failure to accomplish a goal, not being able to control oneself, on any financial situation. How to end suicidal thoughts? Today I am going to tell you some such small tips, which can eliminate your suicidal thoughts. If the thought of suicide ever comes to your mind, then go to a trusted person and tell him everything on your mind. Go to him and cry wholeheartedly. Doing so can reduce the feeling of suicidal ideation. If you don't have someone you trust, find a psychologist or consultant. Tell them everything on your mind. By doing this the burden of your heart will be lightened. Start giving importance to yourself. Write your good qualities on the walls. If you haven't been to a friend in a long time, go to them. By doing this you will feel good and your mind will be calm. Go for a morning walk in the fresh air early in the morning. Instead of putting headphones in your ears, listen to the sounds of the surrounding environment. This will give you a lot of peace and negative thoughts will end from inside you. Add your favorite sport to your routine. Always help the needy and poor, by doing this you feel very light and the smile on their face calms your mind. Do not give importance to anyone more than yourself, because there is no one more important to you than you. The purpose of being born is by eating food, breathing, drinking water, and be happy. Do not make yourself feel alone in any ups and downs of life.

It has been seen that depression is a major cause of suicide. When a person frustrated with life starts finding himself helpless, then he gets trapped in the quagmire of depression. Complicated questions, disappointing answers, and uncertainty take a person to the point where the expectations seem very low. When the situation reaches a critical juncture, the consequences are dire. If there is a need, it should be given timely attention and proper treatment. Work out daily, do yoga and meditation - abstain from alcohol and cigarettes - taste candies or toffees if you like - try to fulfill your hobbies - socialize with people. If possible, share your problem with someone - get the opinion of a psychiatrist. - Avoid painkillers when in pain, consult a doctor - jog or participate in outdoor games - listen to your favourite songs. Remember, don't be sad - Listen to FM Radio. A good diet is also very helpful in dealing with depression: - Eat nutritious food, which is rich in carbohydrates as well as proteins and minerals, such as oats, wheat, etc. cereals, eggs, milk-curd, cheese, green vegetables (beans, spinach, peas, fenugreek, etc.) and seasonal fruits. - Eat things rich in anti-oxidants and vitamin C, such as broccoli, cilantro, spinach, walnuts, raisins, sweet potatoes, berries, blueberries, kiwis, oranges, etc. Include omega-3 in the diet. For this, eat flaxseeds, nuts, canola, soybean, etc. Instead of eating discolored food, focus on colorful food like carrot, tomato, blueberry, orange, etc. - Drink plenty of water. Drink plenty of coconut water, buttermilk, etc. Stress can be relieved through jogging, swimming, and outdoor games. According to yoga guru Surakshit Goswami, this condition can also be dealt with to a great extent through yoga. Before doing this, consult a yoga expert. You can do Surya

Pranayama and Kapalbhati. But do yoga like Tadasana, Katichkrasana, Uttanpadasana, Bharktasana, Bhujangasana, Dhanuasana, Mandukasana under the supervision of a qualified expert. Surya Namaskar is also very helpful in dealing with depression. This is a complete exercise. By doing this, all parts of the body get exercised. Surya Namaskar should be done in the morning in the open facing the rising sun. This gives the body energy and vitamin D. It also gives relief from mental stress. There are a total of 12 steps in this, which have different effects on the body.

A common question during depression is - why is it so bad with me? In such a situation, whenever a friend is very sad, hold his hand or put a hand on his shoulder so that he can be sure that he is not alone. After the breakup, the couple has hundreds of questions for each other. He may harass the ex-partner by phone, chat, or message for repeated answers. As a friend, stop him because the one who quit will never give the right answer. Tell him in talks that he is not the first person in the world, whom someone has left. The world is full of such breakup stories. If any example is present around and he is leading a normal life, then also introduce him. Many times people in trouble seek the help of drugs. Stop drinking alcohol and smoking. Don't give in at all. The unfinished love story of many famous personalities ended in a glass of wine. Often in depression, there is a thought of taking revenge, so do not let the victim be aggressive. Tell him that revenge is not the solution to anything. When to go to the doctor, First of all, symptoms like lack of mood, feeling depressed take the form of depression after delay. If the sadness persists for week-10 days, then see a doctor. Then on his advice, see a psychologist or psychiatrist. It is advisable to see a psychologist at the beginning of the problem and counselling is enough. Psychologists cannot give medicine to the patient. They do not have a medical degree and usually, their job is to counsel patients. At the beginning of the depression, the problem is often resolved by visiting a psychologist, but as the disease progresses, the help of a psychiatrist has to be taken. The psychiatrist also gives medicines to the patient when needed. Apart from an MBBS degree, they also have a specialization in Psychiatry. Suicide cases are increasing continuously all over the world. At present, people are falling prey to depression due to many personal reasons. Some people try to overcome their depression, while some people try to take wrong steps by coming into depression or saying that they take wrong steps. You must have read about many suicide cases in newspapers and news channels, in which more than half of the people commit suicide due to depression. When stress dominates the person in personal or work areas, then he becomes a victim of depression. In such a situation, thoughts of suicide start in the mind of many people.

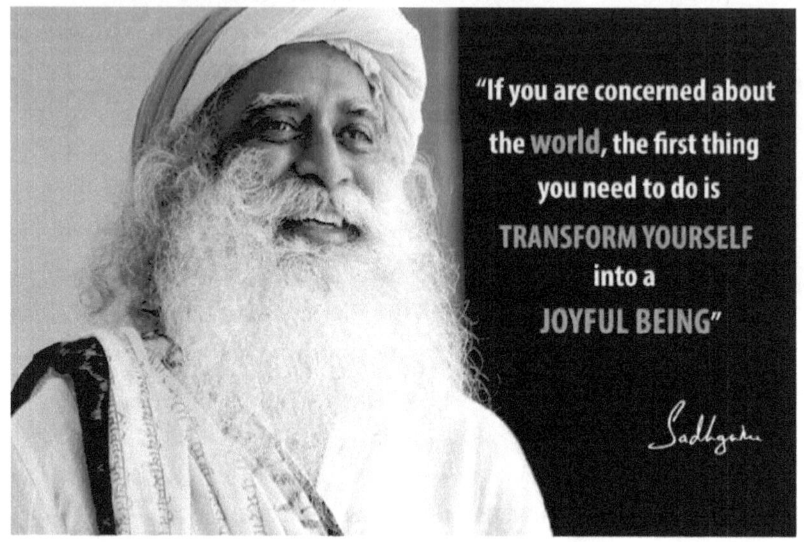
"If you are concerned about
the world, the first thing
you need to do is
TRANSFORM YOURSELF
into a
JOYFUL BEING"

M. RELATIONSHIP BETWEEN HEALTH AND ENVIRONMENT. YOUTHS CAN CHANGE SUCH SITUATIONS.

Everything in the universe is related to the other. Nothing is different. Everything affects everything. Mental-physical health and environment are also linked to each other. There is a need to understand how our environment is related to our health. Health is not just part of disease or disorder. Many factors affect human health, mainly biological, psychological and chemical. These factors are linked to internal and external conditions. The biggest factor influencing health among external factors is the environment. The environment is related to the air we breathe, the water we drink, and the soil in which food is nourished. Every part of it affects us and our health, but the important basis of human health, the environment is facing many questions at this time. The most serious questions are that of pollution, climate change, ecological degradation, and loss of biodiversity. Behind all this, from human activities to the anti-nature character of knowledge-science and technology and the self-centered lifestyle of man. Sweet relationship of health and environment. Our home is a mini-eco-system. If the atmosphere of our home is good that is everyone is happy and filled with positivity we also started feeling good. This is the power of the atmosphere. We all are living in the same environment so if our environment is good means unpolluted and clean then we automatically feel good because of which youths can't search for happiness in other things including addictions. In such a way health and environment are related to each other. Youths are the future so now, it is in the hands of youths to maintain cleanliness in their environment, it is their responsibility that they don't promote pollution. If they implement these habits from now then they can definitely bring change to the environment which can definitely change their future.

They should study health disorders from an individual as well as an environmental point of view. Due to increasing industrialization and advanced industrialization, the natural environment of the earth has been disturbed. This disturbance has unbalanced the natural harmony of nature and, since human life is an integral part of nature, the increasing natural imbalance has also unbalanced human life. It is a truth that today's increasing industrialization and technological development have provided such ultra-modern comforts to man, due to which his life has become unexpectedly simple and comfortable. But it is equally true that due to increasing industrialization and advanced industrialization, the natural environment of the earth has been disturbed. This disturbance has unbalanced the natural harmony of nature and, since human life is an integral part of nature, the increasing natural imbalance has also unbalanced human life. As a result, today's deteriorating environment is affecting human health a lot. Man's health is undoubtedly his great asset because healthy thoughts reside in the body itself. Healthy thoughts have creativity, intensity, and readiness, as well as the ability, not just the will, to get something done. A happy mind resides only in a healthy body, and a satisfied and happy mind has the capacity to have goodwill for mankind and without any discrimination, think about the development of itself, its family, country, and society can do. In such situations, it can be said that the good health of a man is of great importance not only to himself but also to his family, country, and society. Therefore, the adverse effect of the environment on the health of human beings is definitely a matter of concern. While discussing the environment, first of all, we will consider the fact that what the meaning of this word is. It is generally understood that air, water, soil, and trees, and plants together make up the environment. This is true but in a limited sense. Broadly speaking we can say that the whole environment around man, inside and outside the house, everything is a part of the environment. Therefore, if the pollution of water and air can be injurious to human health, at the same time many common household items also contaminate our environment. Exploration, development, and use of environmentally friendly means are necessary to avoid the contamination of smoke which is obviously harming the environment. Plants draw carbon dioxide from the atmosphere, and in return give clean oxygen. Therefore tree plantation should be encouraged for a better environment. Both internal and external factors affect our mental and physical health. Internal factors include problems within the body such as weakened immunity, hormonal imbalances, or a genetic disorder.

Three major external factors are – ultraviolet and radioactive radiation, noise pollution, elements such as carbon monoxide and CFCs. Among the industrial hazards are the chemical hazards of heavy metals, pesticides, and fossil fuel combustion. At the same time, many biological threats like parasites, bacteria, and viruses are also in front of humans. The reason for all this is human activities on earth. Whatever good and bad we share in our ecosystem, it eventually comes back to us. The disturbance of ecological balance is most clearly reflected first in the quality of water and air pollution and in extreme conditions. At the same time, radiation also gradually affects human health. Decreasing biodiversity is pushing life towards a perpetual crisis. The relationship between physical-mental health and the environment is complex. Human beings are also a little careless in understanding this. We look forward to irrefutable evidence in the direction of understanding this relationship. On the other hand, it is not sensible to reason with nature, it is a relation involving emotion; It is a matter of common sense. If a bad environment harms human health, then a good environment can also be healthy. A healthy society requires the development of strong ecosystems, economic growth, sustainable poverty reduction, an environment of human well-being, and a tendency to conserve resources. The environment includes all the forces that function without the individual. Broadly speaking, the environment has two sides: first physical, second social.

The environment can include all those external factors that act on the individual as life begins. Lamarck considers the ability of an individual to adapt to the environment as important, while Darwin considers the survival of the fittest to be the life principle. It was around these two philosophies that man's attitude towards nature developed. While the first philosophy nurtures a lifestyle of co-existence and co-existence with nature, the second philosophy is that of conquering nature. This tendency towards the illusion of control over nature continued to fuel the development of science and technology. The resultant indiscriminate urbanization and industrialization compounded the environmental problems. Occult activities brought about the conditions of climate change. This led to global warming. This crisis, arising from the excess of certain types of gases in the atmosphere, is at the root of all environmental crises. Today it is not only harming the environment but it is affecting every aspect of human life. The measure of every activity on earth is the health of the environment, whose common unit of measurement is carbon-foot-prints. How are all the living beings on earth conducting their life? Is he living a lifestyle of co-existence and co-operation with nature or is he self-centered inventing facilities to conquer nature and excessive consumption? Carbon footprints are a marker of our actions. Global warming increases the temperature of the earth, which affects agriculture on a large scale. Crop rotation is erratic, productivity decreases, resulting in increased food scarcity and manifested in the form of starvation and malnutrition. This directly affects health and disturbs the overall lifecycle. The number of animals, birds, and plants starts decreasing. has adverse effects on human health. The frequency of natural calamities like floods, droughts, hurricanes, cyclones, earthquakes, and landslides increases. The displaced population is vulnerable to famine, starvation, social inequalities, and mental diseases. Their resettlement creates additional problems by creating discontent among the local population. The world is affected by natural calamities like floods, earthquakes, hurricanes, cyclones, and super cyclones, droughts. Technological and industrial advances in modern models of development have qualitatively increased environmental hazards.

N. YOUTHS TOWARDS RESEARCH AND INNOVATION. IS IT A NEED OR NOT?

The development of any country is associated with the progress of its people. In outlook of this, it becomes necessary that Youths should get involved in Research and innovation. Research and investigation composition should play an important part in every aspect of life. A country can progress on the path of development only when information and knowledge grounded terrain is created for its unborn generation and acceptable coffers for exploration with research and innovation. The wars of modern times are very different from the wars of the late nineteenth century. Modern wars do not take place in human beings, they are fought mechanically, even with the help of automatic weapons. To do so, the soldiers have to have great support for the country's science and equipment. For such content, of course, the nation has to be self-sufficient in all respects and for that, the industries of the country have to be developed. Only when a nation is superior to the enemy in this respect is it convinced that we can defend ourselves by repelling an enemy attack. That is, we must be ahead of the enemy nation in all respects, mainly in arms and the industries that make them. The progress and updating of industries are impossible without continuous research. From this point of view, it is clear that any nation needs industrial research as well and we youngsters can play a great role here, isn't it? In addition to defence, the nation's economic system needs to be strong in addition to weapons. Things are necessary. Good food grains require a lot of seeds, fertilizers, water, machinery, etc. For self-sufficiency of raw materials, the mining industry, chemical engineering, etc. should be developed. Instead of having to import raw materials from abroad, it is necessary to make the alternative raw materials available in the country to use in the factories. I think it can be the solution. Ultimately, increasing exports by producing high quality but relatively inexpensive items will not be possible without better development of the industry but taking into consideration we should go with Ecology as well.

The development of industries means the expansion of existing industries and the opening up of new industries. According to the Indian Science and Research and Development Industry Report 2019, India is among the top-ranking countries in the field of basic research. The world's third-largest scientific and technical manpower is also in India. Are you getting it the youngsters of INDIA you really have a great opportunity? Various research works are carried out through research laboratories run by the Council of Scientific and Industrial Research (CSIR). India ranks seventh among the leading countries in the field of science and technology research. India has become the fourth major country in the region after Japan, Britain, and the US by making a powerful supercomputer named PRATYUSH for weather forecasting and monitoring. India also ranks third in the world in terms of research on nanotechnology. We are ranked 57th in the Global Innovation Index. India is reaching the state of brain gain from brain drain and Indian scientists working abroad are returning home. India is emerging as an applied research destination and over the years we have increased investment in research and development. India is fast emerging in research, innovation, and development. Don't you think this is only possible due to youths of the nation and still young minds of Indian experts? Isn't it an opportunity for we youngsters to contribute even more for the betterment of humanity, society, and National welfare?

See readers, There are two types of research benefits. The first is the short-term benefit and the second is a long-term benefit. In the first case, the actual amount of benefit is less and the research done for it is less labour, time, and cost. Electric appliances for rubbing or shaving limbs or housewife's cooking appliances that reduce the hassle in the house e.g. Searches fall into the first category. The second type of research takes a lot of time, even a few years, and it takes a long time to actually benefit from the results. Aircraft, missiles, missiles, space travel overcoming the earth's gravity, solar reduction of satellite power supply, synthetic fibers like polyester are all examples of long-term benefits. We can say radical research mainly adds to the knowledge of the human universe, industrial research has worldly benefits. His comforts have increased, his daily labour has decreased. Medicines have become more abundant and cheaper, health has improved and life expectancy has also increased. This shows the importance of industrial research in the progress of any nation. In the field of science and technology, the number of teachers should be increased so that the basic problem like lack of teachers in universities can be overcome. There is also a need for a proper institutional framework, suitable infrastructure, desired projects, and substantial investment in science and technology institutions to enhance R&D activities, investment participation in mega-science projects for the creation of R&D infrastructure in India and abroad. There is a need to provide opportunities for talented students to pursue careers in science, research, and innovation. In view of all this, a policy has to be made in which emphasis can promote scientific Reformation to all sections of the society and enhance the skills for the applications of Research among the youth from all Garmin to District to state to nation.

The government is also making efforts to promote innovation in the field of science and technology, still more efforts are needed in this direction. There is a need to create better national facilities in the field of science and technology to promote participation in research work. Appropriate programs should be undertaken to promote technology sharing between the Central and the States along with the district level. You can also suggest ideas to our Indian government for betterment creating awareness towards national welfare. You as a youth can participate in many innovative ideas and programs of government such as Connect with PM and Namo app facilities. It can make a difference. Your ideas as youngsters can really help the to the nation for achieving great heights. Start thinking about it and even you can be the innovator of upcoming research achievements of India.

O. WOMEN EMPOWERMENT

We are now in the 21st century but still, we are discussing about women's empowerment and their rights regarding education, safety, economics, politics, and many more. Women have become the pillars of society by playing various roles with ease in daily life. Sometimes she is a loving daughter or loving mother or sometimes a capable companion. In this way, she is handling all the relationships with the utmost skills and tenderness.

Even so, women are still beyond the reach of the average person. Also, women are victims of a great deal of social inequality, economic dependence, and other social oppression. From time immemorial these restrictions on women have hampered their personal and professional development. If we are talking about youth empowerment for reformation then women's empowerment is the most important part of that because women's empowerment and gender equality in our society will be helpful to ensure sustainable development in our country.

We are celebrating festivals like Navratri, Durga pooja, Kanya Pooja, Laxmi pooja but in reality, women get tamed, harassed, abused, kidnapped, and raped every single day. According to Hillary Clinton "Human rights are women's rights and women's rights are human rights, once and for all"

But in reality, these are just lines... Many times they are sexually and mentally assaulted at their working place or public places like the bus stop, market, malls, and sometimes in their home by their own people. We are living in a society where the way of thinking of people is like the work of women's is only handling her home and being a parent and if she wants to get rid of that's and get apart from her comfort zone then many times she has to face underestimation and harassment by her own society.

'But if she can then she will, and she definitely will'

Empowerment is not just about educational freedom but also about the greet of what she wants to become whether it is economically, socially, educationally, or politically.

Education is the basic and most prior right of all people even girl's and women's but still, in some areas, women's are restricted but education is the key part of empowerment because girls who are educated can pursue meaningful work and can contribute to their countries' economy later in life. Many women are just unaware of their rights but the right to education on the basics of non-discrimination and equality is a recognized right under human rights law. Provisions relating to gender equality in education can be found in both general and specific international treaties as well as treaties concluded in most regions of the world.

We have knowledge about Mahatma Phule and Savitribai Phule who fought for girls' education and their rights. 'Savitribai Phule' is the best example of how one woman can fight for their rights and how bold she can become. If she is a loving mother then at a time she can become 'Durga'.

Being financially and economically stable is the need and one of the unspeakable wishes of every woman. Women's started their own businesses and worked tirelessly to prove that they are as adept and successful in the entrepreneurial space as their male counterparts. If we take a look at the dedication and intelligence of women then we understand that they are adorable in their own way 'Mission Mangal ' is the best example of women's power and their presence of mind in every worst situation they had faced. If we talk about the women who work under 'Google ' then we realize that what kind of facilities they will provide during maternity leave or any other family situations. Because they respect the work of women and their dedication. In our Indian laws, girls or women have their rights about their properties such as the daughter shall remain a coparcener throughout life, irrespective of whether her father is alive or not. Daughters must be given equal rights as son's, but it doesn't mean that they became economically stable, giving them equal opportunities in all fields will become them economically stable, if we want to know the strength, boldness, dedication, perseverance, and patience then we should think about the time when one woman give the birth to the children because giving birth is the second most painful thing in the world after burning alive. At that time every muscle of the body gets stretched but she faces all that pain.

She plays a vital role in every place of progress whether it is in education, farming, caretaking, being a doctor or being a politician, or surviving as a soldier.

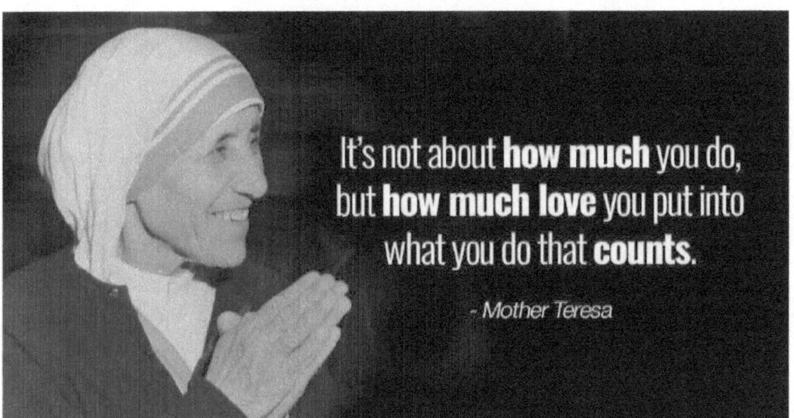
It's not about **how much** you do,
but **how much love** you put into
what you do that **counts**.
- Mother Teresa

P. Youths Mindset? Is Sex attraction or porn curiosity affecting youths a lot?

Watching Porn and sex videos are rapidly increasing in youths. I am not so intelligent to write on this topic. But it is becoming an addiction for youths and in excess proportion, it is leading to wrong mindsets and adverse effects on our cultured land. I agree that changing lifestyle is giving birth to new habits among the youth. Also, the youths in society are moving towards modernity but, don't you think some distracted and addicted youths are forgetting its values and running behind new habits. One of these habits that the Indian youth has inculcated is the addiction to watching porn. While adult youth in Western countries are feeling the ill effects of excessive online porn, experts now warn that Indian teens are also at risk. According to sex and applied science experts, sex is such a mystery that teenagers are curious about it but it is affecting very rapidly and creating danger for youths. According to my observation, many times group of young teenagers standing together are talking about porn. I am not saying it is totally wrong but it is affecting very badly on developing mindsets of budding youths. This makes me write on this topic and create awareness highlighting some points.

Porn addiction is often overlooked as a minor issue. Neither the victim of this addiction nor the people around the addict understand its seriousness. It is made into a mood swing or a habit by taking it as an in-and-out thing. The attitude of porn addicts towards the family also changes. He gets cut off from all kinds of roles in the family. If it increases a lot, then the victims of this addiction can do from rape to murder. Victims of porn addiction can even take the step of suicide by becoming a victim of self-incrimination or guilt. From college life to joining a job, almost everyone watches porn but not necessarily all become addicted. It is like not every person who drinks alcohol or smokes cigarettes in college life for a few days becomes addicted to it but some of them are unable to leave it and get caught in its clutches. - There can be many reasons for this. Sometimes it depends on the environment and sometimes on the upbringing. The kind of exposure, so will the attitude. There can also be genetic reasons for addiction. But what kind of addiction will be, it will be decided by the circumstances. Before understanding porn addiction, it is important to understand addiction. Getting used to anything to such an extent, due to which normal life is disturbed, comes under the category of addiction. The reason for every addiction is different, some have a food addiction and some have tea. Even when the habit of watching porn reaches such an extent that personal and professional life starts getting affected by it, then it should be understood that porn addiction has started. It can be understood in such a way that the victim of porn addiction is always in the quest to watch porn. He likes loneliness. He doesn't want to miss any opportunity to watch porn anytime, anywhere. Due to getting lost in the thoughts of porn all the time, the victim of addiction is neither able to think of any new thing nor is able to do anything by planning. People around him do not pay much attention to it considering it as a change of habit and the victim of this addiction goes on drowning in his addiction. Watching more porn when personal and private life starts getting disturbed because of watching porn, then understand that you are crossing the limit. Often porn watchers watch porn late in the night and because of this, they remain sluggish for the rest of the day. There is no time for their work, no time for rest. There is only one purpose in life: to watch as much porn as possible. If you stop watching porn for some reason, you get confused and do not feel like doing any work. - Continuing to watch porn despite being physically and mentally disturbed. - Masturbating more often - Disinterest towards your partner - Significant changes in sexual behavior such as becoming aggressive, not caring about your partner's feelings - Using porn as a tool to escape from all the troubles and tensions in the world Doing. For example, if there is a little tension, I have watched porn, if the mood is good then I have seen porn, etc. Nowadays access to it has become easy through social media and websites. But most of the answers turn out to be pornography. I this all the negative and adverse effects are due to ignorance about Sex education. Everything people need to know about healthy sex first. Porn is a mixed form of it. There are fears that readily available online porn could lead young people to risky sexual behaviour, especially in a country with the largest population of youth in the world. The habit of watching porn depends on one's personality, where desire is not controlled, where the need is insatiable and behaviour is compulsive. When youths reach this stage, they need immediate treatment. Basically, you can start with Meditation. There are basically two types of methods used in its treatment: Psychotherapy and Medicine - In psychotherapy, the patient is given 12 counselling sessions. - About 2 sessions are given every week. As a medicine, drugs to reduce depression and relieve mental problems are given. This happens only in very serious cases. Counselling often gives relief to the patient. If there is an addict in the house, do not leave him alone. In this way, a victim of addiction will not be able to watch porn. If possible, take the addicted person on long walks. Start doing yoga and exercise. By doing this the mind will move away from porn. - Take the porn addict person towards his hobby. If you are fond of music then gift a music CD and if you are fond of reading then books.

Even Kids have access to adult content at an early age due to easy access to the Internet and media. Access to such things through other students in the school. - Younger curiosity - Parents being open about things and giving kids unlimited access to gadgets. - Spending less time in outdoor games. Instead of indoor games like ludo and chess, send kids to outdoor games. Tell them about the benefits of it. If possible, play outdoor games with them like jogging, football or badminton yourself. Outdoor games are not only good for the physical and mental development of children, but they keep children busy so that they neither have time nor energy for things like porn. Parents should keep the use of mobile and computers under control in front of children. It is necessary to give them an understanding from childhood that these gadgets are for essential work and not for entertainment.

Children learn the wrong use of these gadgets from home. Keep child lock on your mobile, desktop, and laptop. Even if you give gadgets to children, control them. For this, website filters and password protection can be used. I think parents can really make difference here in such situations. Be a Role Model, Parents are the role models of kids. It is often seen that parents start a discussion on any topic in front of them, considering their children to be ignorant. This type of behaviour increases the curiosity of the children and they try to get to the bottom of what they have heard. It is becoming a common thing nowadays for children or teenagers to visit porn websites. Which has many disadvantages and the biggest loss that happens within them is the creation of a distorted view of sex. If you are suffering from such a problem, Maybe you don't have any time-passing habit, that's when your attention goes more towards porn. In such a situation, it is very important that you start a new habit as soon as possible. This will keep your mind engaged and you will also be able to get rid of porn addiction.

It may happen that you are unable to stop watching pornography and other behaviours associated with it such as masturbation despite trying to avoid it repeatedly? Do you need to watch porn? Do you crave it? Do you become angry if someone confronts you about porn use? Do you have to keep watching more explicit porn to gain satisfaction? Even in simple acts of physical expressions of love with a significant other like holding their hand or sharing a kiss? Have you stopped being involved with your friends or family because of the need to watch porn? Have you kept it a secret from loved ones?

If your answer is yes to more than a few of these questions, it's time to seriously evaluate how porn can negatively affect your life and your relationships with loved ones. You are in danger and you really need meditation and proper consultancy. If you want to change, it's time to reach out to someone who cares and understands you. If no one is there such. Go with meditation, yoga, exercise, and the best way books of the world. Here are some ways you can fight and avoid porn addiction. This addiction grabs you in secret when you are alone, and when you believe, no one will ever know and then you start your game. Trust me find the best person, it is a friend, a parent, or even an accountability group, find someone you can trust to be open and honest about your addiction. My best suggestion is to go and directly share everything with your parents. If you really wanna get rid of this addiction on your own, you may fail. Not discouraging you. But the best way is not to go on your own and not trying to go with it alone. Confide in someone who loves and cares for you. Have safeguards in place on your phone or electronics or however you access porn. Buy a flip phone if you have to.

Wherever you are the most tempted and whenever you are the most tempted, replace that time with another activity that also releases good chemicals in the brain like exercising. Keep the door open. Put your phone outside of your bedroom if you are tempted at night. Do whatever it takes and then it is easily possible for you to get rid out of this. If you are addicted to porn I think, you should go to professional counselling. If you have tried everything you can and the clutches of pornography still haven't released you, there is no shame in going to counselling or seeking out group therapy. Pornography has neurological side effects and can be treated. Find help and you can win yourself. Don't be ashamed, it is a natural process and everyone has to go and deal with it.

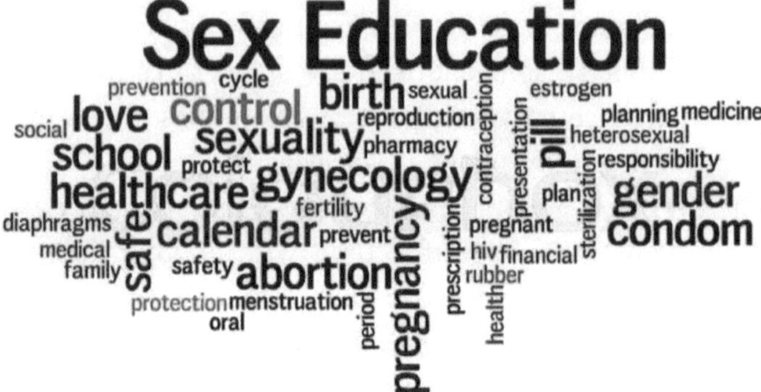
Sex Education
prevention
cycle
birth
sexual
estrogen
social
love
control
reproduction
planning medicine
school
sexuality
pharmacy
pill
heterosexual
protect
contraception
presentation
responsibility
healthcare
gynecology
plan
gender
diaphragms
fertility
prevent
pregnant
condom
medical
calendar
safe
sterilization
family
safety
abortion
prescription
hiv financial
rubber
protection
menstruation
period
pregnancy
health
oral

Q. EMPLOYABILITY, UNEMPLOYMENT, AND ENTREPRENEURSHIP.

Our India is called a golden bird, but if we consider the recent scenario, it comes under observation that even after so many years of independence, our country continues to fight with one or the other problems every day, isn't it? The major problem we observe here is unemployment. People have hands, but no work, people are in the phase of training, but no job, people have plans and enthusiasm, but there is no opportunity. Unemployment is a curse for society. This not only has a bad effect on the individuals but unemployment also affects the whole society. Unemployment is a very serious issue not only in India but all over the world. There are hundreds and thousands of people here who do not have employment. Being unemployed means being unable to get employment in spite of being complete with ability and education. This problem arises when there is a shortage of work and there is an excess of workers. Unemployed is called a person who wants to work at the prevailing wage rate in the market but is unable to get work. The definition of unemployment varies from country to country. Due to being in the shackles of dependence for many years, India is not able to develop at the expected pace in this sector many more developments are yet to come and our government is always in the positive actions for this. This is also resulting in governments facing many great hurdles to establishing themselves self-reliantly and powerfully on the world stage. The Indian economy, even after so many years of independence, is in utter collapse. Even though our governments strive to improve the standard of living of the people and provide them suitable employment, but the ground reality is that most of our population is forced to sleep hungry and remain without education due to unemployment. There is no facility available to such at ground level. In such circumstances, the importance of our governments, which make policies to eliminate poverty and unemployment from the root, can be gauged automatically. Increasingly, the unemployment figure has taken such a terrible and frightening form that it is a big challenge for us to face it. However, with the introduction of new economic policies such as privatization and liberalization in India in the early nineties, India's employment situation received little support. Due to these policies, many such industries developed, due to which there a decrease in the figures was related to unemployment.

Due to economic liberalization and globalization, even multinational companies, which helped a lot in improving the standard of living of our youth, were able to spread their feet in India. But this development has been limited to urban areas only. The development of the real India, which lives in the villages, was allowed to remain neglected, as a result of which the employment situation in the villages is very deplorable. The biggest reason behind these situations is that after the attainment of independence, when the governance of the country came into the hands of Indian leaders, considering industrialization and development of cities as their priority, all the development plans focused on urban life only. A very less important place was ensured in his plans for the development of villages and for improving the standard of living of the people living in rural areas.

India is a country with a very large population. The faster the population is growing, the faster the economic level of individuals and employment opportunities are falling at a faster rate. A developing nation like India can't employ such a large population. The number of people working day and night in search of employment far exceeds the number of resources and opportunities available. This is the reason that even today most of the youth are compelled to lead a life in unemployment. The government is also serious about this issue and a new cabinet committee has been constituted for this. When the manpower working in a country is more and people do not get work at the prevailing wages even after agreeing to work, then such a condition is called unemployment. The existence or non-existence of unemployment depends on the constant ratio between the demand for and supply of labour. There are also many Challenges in Skill Development, on one hand, we have lakhs of graduates who have passed out from colleges with degrees and are unemployed due to lack of relevant skills. On the other hand, we have many skilled candidates who are looking for employment but the industry still wants them to graduate at least. The main question from this situation is "Where do the candidates go?" At one end, we have degree-holders who are unemployed and at the other end, we have our skilled candidates but without formal degrees. For a young country with possibly the largest number of job seekers entering the labour market every month, it is unfortunate that education policy pays little attention to skill development.

If we consider Entrepreneurship, Whether it is a business that produces products or a business that provides services, small entrepreneurs face many difficulties throughout their business life. It is advisable to prepare ahead of time so as not to hinder the expansion of the business. A long-lasting and successful business requires hard work and dedication. Once you know what problems may arise, it is possible to plan for them. For small entrepreneurs, the company registration process is lengthy and costly. Raising funds or finance is a big problem in small businesses. It is difficult to start a business without adequate funding. Loans are not readily available, loans are not approved due to poor financial conditions, or there is no qualification required to take a loan. In such a situation you have to take a loan at a higher interest rate which in turn worsens your financial situation and qualifications. The terms and conditions of the banks are not flexible and it becomes difficult to run the industry.

The problem of unemployment is taking a very formidable form. The problem of unemployment is like a stigma on the head of the nation. Today, the problem of unemployment is increasing continuously in our country, which is direct proof of our unemployed youth. There are so many youths around us who have achieved very high level degrees but they are still wandering here and there in search of employment. In search of jobs, people keep circling the offices every day and are engaged in searching for jobs according to their qualifications through advertisements given in newspapers and the internet, but they do not get employment. The biggest reason for unemployment in India is its huge population which demands a large number of jobs every year which the government and authorities are unable to provide. So there are also many types of unemployment, which include many things like educated unemployment, uneducated unemployment, seasonal unemployment, underemployment and disguised unemployment, and many more. People engaged in agriculture get employment at the time of plowing, sowing, harvesting, etc., but as soon as the agricultural work is over, then the people engaged in agriculture become unemployed. Apart from this, some unemployed people can also get fine wages, but still, these people do not want to work as beggars, fake sadhus, etc. because of unemployment. The growing problem of unemployment is continuously becoming a challenge to our progress, peace, and stability. There are many reasons for unemployment in our country.

Due to the proportion of the increase in population, there is a lack of jobs and there is very little increase in opportunities, due to which unemployment is increasing. Mechanization has also taken away employment from the hands of innumerable people and made them unemployed because one machine can handle the work of many workers. It results in, a very large number of people are becoming unemployed. Gandhiji used to say - 'Our country does not need more production, but more production by hands.' He encouraged small industries instead of big machines. His symbol was the spinning wheel. But most people did not understand the essence of that truth in the glare of modernity. The result was that the machines kept increasing, the hands became empty. An army of useless has gathered. The major reason for this is our education system. There has been no change in our education system for many years.

Our education system is also faulty for unemployment. There is a lack of business-oriented education. Due to a lack of practical or technical education, the student remains unemployed after completing his education. Illiteracy prevalent in India is also the main reason for unemployment. In today's machine age there is a need for educated and skilled and trained persons. We give very special importance to literacy development in our education system. Vocational and technical education is neglected. Big businessmen and companies get loans up to billions of rupees easily from the government, but loans are not given to the common person to set up small-scale industries, due to which small-scale industries are not able to develop and poverty in the country is spread.

The solution to every problem lies in its causes. Therefore, if the above-mentioned reasons are effectively curbed, then the problem of unemployment can be solved to a great extent. Vocational education, promotion of small-scale industries, control over mechanization, search for new employment opportunities, control over the population, etc., should be implemented expeditiously. Unless there is a proper solution to this problem, neither there will be happiness and peace in the society nor will the orderly and disciplined structure of the nation be established. Skill development schemes can solve the problem of unemployment in the future. We Indians have to empower ourselves through knowledge and new inventions so that big companies around the world can know our strength and they invest in India and start their own companies. This will give new career opportunities to the people of our country and will help our country to develop. Recently, the government has also started many types of schemes to take the youth of India forward like Pradhan Mantri Kaushal Vikas Yojana, Mudra Loan the scheme, Housing Scheme, Beti Bachao- Beti Padhao Abhiyan, Sukanya Samridhi Yojana etc. People should join these schemes of the government and educate their coming generation through these schemes so that they can become the future of our country India. We can say that the problem of unemployment in India has reached a critical stage. But, now the government and local authorities have taken this problem seriously and are working on it to reduce unemployment. Also, to solve the unemployment issue completely, we have to deal with the main issue of unemployment which is the huge population of India. Unemployment gives rise to many problems like corruption, terrorism, unrest, disturbance, riots, theft, dacoity, kidnapping, etc. In order to harness the power and energy of the youth, it is necessary to get proper education and then proper guidance, otherwise, the youth go astray and evils spread in the society.

In the name of development and industrialization, our welfare governments do not shy away from acquiring land for multinational companies and big capitalists from poor agricultural farmers at very low prices. They say that the acquired land is barren, while the reality is that the land used to provide employment to that farmer and his entire family, how can it be barren? Our governments give an assurance that once the industry is established, one person from the family of the farmers, whose land has been acquired, will be given a job in the same industry. On the contrary, till the establishment of the industry, the farmer maintains the family with the amount of compensation and when he does not get any kind of job, he is forced to commit suicide to get rid of the life of poverty and misery. The problem of rising unemployment is directly related to corruption. As corruption is flourishing, the amount of employment is decreasing. The government is running various employment-related schemes to raise the standard of living of the people in rural areas, trying to make recruitment transparent in government and private institutions. But in reality, all these efforts are hollow and misleading. Rising unemployment, overpopulation, widespread illiteracy, and corruption are giving equal strength to the rising unemployment in India. For this reason, the number of criminal offenses in the country is also increasing day by day. If serious efforts are made to reduce any one of these factors, then it can be easy to eliminate the problem of unemployment.

The number of educated unemployed has also reached in crores. Before the introduction of neo-liberal economic policies three decades ago, the share of government jobs in the gross employment in the country was two percent, but after the liberal economic policies, due to the privatization of various sectors, employment opportunities are continuously decreasing. In such a situation, the question arises that is it only the responsibility of the government to provide employment to all the unemployed youth? The government alone cannot create all the jobs, that's why Standup, Startup India and Mudra schemes are being implemented to increase the spirit of entrepreneurship, yet at present, the employment opportunities with the government are very limited. The private sector wants to operate with less labour and invests where it sees a profit. On the other hand, the loss of traditional and ancestral occupations in the villages is also a matter of concern as the educated youth no longer see any potential in these occupations. It is meaningless to imagine building a clean, happy and advanced country until all the youth of the country get work according to their ability and requirement. There are ample employment opportunities in less populated countries, but due to the increasing population in India, unemployment is increasing. Then what is the solution for creating employability? If vocational skills and education are integrated, India as a country has a huge demographic dividend that can create a huge pool of skilled professionals and become the skill capital of the world. How can India create a large skilled labour force? Vocational skills should be very closely linked with the education system and need to be started in the early years of education. Every student should be exposed to some basic skills and some specific ones which they can choose to learn as they go down the education path. The initial few years should be spent in providing an overview and preparing students for what skill set they want and will be good at. Teach him a particular skill over the next few years, such that when he completes his graduation, he is ready for employment in the given field. In general, we have been teaching mostly through classrooms, but four classroom learning modes – on-campus, on-site, online, and on-the-job should become the way of learning. for the duration of each class. The schedule and structure can be customized to the students based on their class, skill set, and background.

A National Credit Mechanism may be put in place which will recognize the efficient education of students to take place in parallel with their formal education. This will not only help in building confidence to acquire vocational skills but will also increase the social enlightenment for training. To sustain the student's interest in learning, there is a need for changes in the curriculum, infrastructure, and content. Teachers and lecturers in schools and colleges play the most important role in shaping the careers of their students. It is essential for teachers to keep themselves advanced on the subjects and skills they teach students. How India can solve this problem? We often hear industries complaining about not being job-ready and academics speak about helping industry prepare the workforce of the future. The best way to engage industry during a student's education is to integrate classroom teaching with on-the-job learning. This will provide ample opportunities for all the stakeholders to understand each other's capabilities, strengths and help in overcoming the weak areas. Subjects such as behavioural skills, communication, IT, teamwork, analytical ability, etc. can be developed for the students from the early classes and then they can be introduced to trade specific skills from class 9, which can be learned from the undergraduate years and onwards can also be continued. Learning new skills and gaining knowledge is a life-long activity. It is not something to be set aside for years of education.

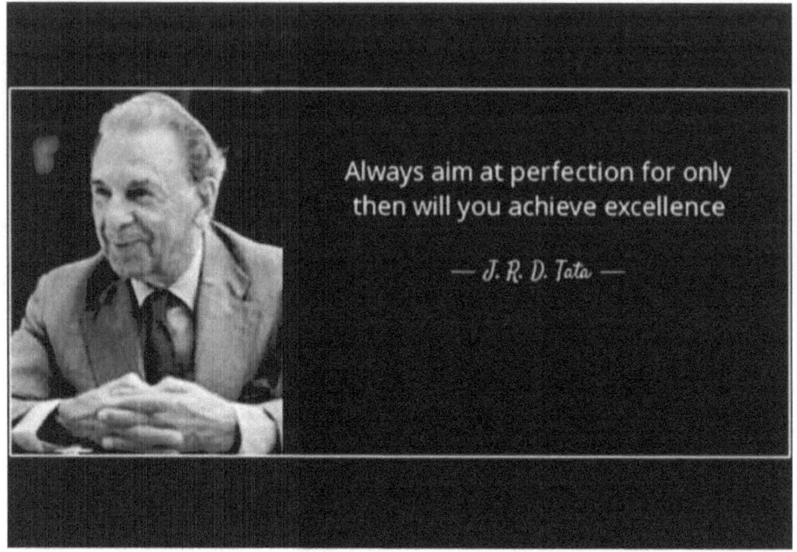
Always aim at perfection for only
then will you achieve excellence
— J. R. D. Tata —

R. THE COMPETITION + THE PRESSURE + THE FAILURE = CURRENT YOUTHS.

It's been years since when India has witnessed and yet witnessed the condition of the country's youths not only the good ones but also the bad ones too. Every year the percentage is counted of how much is the percentage of students attempting that one step which end their lives. The country had also recorded the limit of the youth's mentality and level of pressure and anxiety. No matter what is the pressure about, let it be of studies or any other aspects. But they have now set up their minds in a way that leads to harm themselves. The future youths of India are sometimes giving up somewhere they shouldn't be. How can we encourage them? What should be their mindsets and step needs to be taken? And what are the main reason that is making them do so? These three questions need an answer.

'Youth', a period of 13 to 35 years on which their overall life depends on. This is the stage when an individual needs to know about their purpose of existence in life. Along with this, they should make themselves ready for upcoming challenges that are faced in this period. Even a small challenge, in turn, results in huge reform. One needs to be up to date with their strengths and weakness. Not all youths will be bound to cross this face very easily. There might be thousands of ups and downs including tons of pros and cons which they may have to deal with. With the growing population, there is also an increase in competition of youths. The competition is good, it should be but not that much, which starts affecting our personal life. Especially in the case of students, there are in time more serious and confident about their hard work and expectations about their result at a particular time.

> *"Tasks may be difficult at times,*
> *One is bound, should know to climb.*
> *Hills of ultimatum is the eternal test,*
> *If you win, you go, if you lose, you're blessed.*
> *Because it's time to plan the quest."*

The above lines hold deep meaning. It is bound that an individual is surrounded by summons and they might be indeed difficult too. But one who wins it is perfect, but who doesn't can make himself a perfectionist. So, dear mates, it's time to go back and start planning to reach the heights of success. There will be competition at every step of life, instead of giving up, cope up with competitors and I'm sure, it would be a grand success. Sometimes, when there is everything going accordingly, we see something on social media about our near ones especially friends and some relatives. It's peer pressure. We sometimes think or realize that we're lacking somewhere in life because of that one thing we see on social media. Is there any need for it? Why should we hurt ourselves when it's not meant for us? Thus, it all leads us to a change in behaviour and makes us feel lacking somewhere even if we aren't. And then the thing of 'Ego' and 'Hatred' rise up which destroys the dignity we achieved for years. Then sometimes life hits hard so hard that all that craziness breaks down in seconds. It is rightly said, "Peer Pressure can either make you or break you. Positive peer pressure will lead you to your dreams and negative peer pressure will lead to your nightmares. Do choose wisely." Also, not all positive peer pressure would be trustworthy, and not all negative peer pressure intends to destroy you. Do observe minutely.

> *"It's prone hard to deal with fear,*
> *They know, aspects would appear.*
> *Fear of failure is indeed challenged,*
> *And so, the morale needs to be raised."*

Fear of failure is the most difficult thing one needs to pass with. In the case of students, they need moral support in every way possible. They should know a thing that their hard work matters. Their every effort prevails. Their every step of optimism is considered. But only at a certain limit, because thinking only through one way won't do. They should know to deal with pessimism and work more on optimism. These days, mostly in exam times, we often hear, students, getting depressed because of failure in results. They find themselves lacking in their efforts. But it's wrong. Getting depressed leads to harm to the brain. The mentality converts in the same point. And sometimes, in every act we blame ourselves. The reason behind most attempting activities is fear of failure. What if this fear condition in India will result in trauma issues? In all exams, one day before we see in the news, someone attempt suicide. And what's the reason? Fear of failing and the consequences that would be dealt with. Why? One starts thinking about what society would say after that. Though it doesn't matter who speaks what? It's not about them, it's about us that at least we tried. It's the work of everyone to pass comments, they shouldn't be.

In India, according to National Crime Records Bureau (NCRB), it has become prevalent that now in every hour a student attempts suicide, and the number of such cases reached an estimated 28 per day. It's the saddest thing that India is witnessing and has now become a major issue. John Keats once said "Don't be discouraged by a failure. It can be a positive experience. Failure is, in a sense, the highway to success, in as much as every discovery of what is false leads us to seek earnestly after what is true, and every fresh experience points out some form of error which we shall afterward carefully avoid."

SECTION-2

EMPOWERING SOCIAL REFORMATION

Youth is a very Major and Important part of any nation. A nation that is full of energetic, inquisitive, and hardworking youth and the ability to provide them ample opportunities for work forms a strong base for its development. If we consider, why there is a need for social Reformation? There may be many reasons for this. It can help to acquire knowledge and skills for their personal and professional development. It can help to explore their interests. It can help to recognize the potential hidden, it can help in social, Youth, and rural development that indirectly or directly impacts National Welfare. The Government of India also aims at social and youth-led development. Instead of sitting idle, youth should play an active role in the development and progress of the country. To encourage and empower young minds, the government of the country has started the National Youth Policy which is really amazing. Its aim is to potentially direct the youth in the right direction which will help in strengthening the nation as a whole. Several education programs have also been started in the country to ensure that every child gets an education. The Indian government does not discriminate on gender. With the intention of empowering girls in the country, the government has started the Beti Bachao Beti Padhao program. The Department of Youth Affairs is also actively involved in the empowerment of youth. It has taken several initiatives to enhance the leadership qualities and other skills of the youth in the country. When the youth of the country will make full use of their skills and potential then the country will definitely develop and progress and it will get a new identity across the world. A nation that focuses on its social reformation and youth reformation can empower through various initiatives and programs is moving in the right direction.

Yes, it can really make a difference. India is working to build strong and intelligent youth and you as a youth can contribute greatly towards it. But anyhow, we still have a long run to go on. Youth contributes the most to improving society and building the nation. The youth are trying their best to make this line 'Mera Bharat Mahan' meaningful. The attitude of a large number of youth towards the rapid change in the society is turning towards achieving success through work and labour rather than shortcuts. The future is in youth's hands. To make the lines of 'My India great' meaningful, the youth will have to take the initiative. Youth will get a chance only when corruption ends. The first solution for this is to choose an honest and development-oriented person through elections. The vision is that India should become the biggest power in the world. For this, you need to do all your work with honesty and sincerity. Do it yourself before expecting others. Everyone should get equal opportunities and everyone's hard work should be respected and yes then it will for sure lead to social reformation. The vision is, everyone in the country should have employment according to their qualifications, so that crime can be reduced. I think it is necessary to pay more attention to the education of youths as well as girl students. An only educated society will accelerate the pace of development of the country. I think youths also have to sincerely try to achieve their goals to achieve their dreams. I think the great leaders and saints talks and literature created by them can play a very important role in Social youth and nature reformation. Specifically, when we talk about youths, the thoughts of Swami Vivekanand always play a great role. Swami Vivekananda's thinking is not about any particular class but to take the whole world towards upliftment. In today's deteriorating social situation, the young generation needs to assimilate their ideas, only then the youth will be able to take society and the country towards progress.

Youth are the leaders of the country, so they have to understand this responsibility. Today most of the youth all over the world are leaving their country's land and going to another place in view of luxury and convenience. Due to this, there are problems in nation-building. If there is a huge migration of youth, it not only shows the incompetence of that nation. Which cannot give enough resources to its youth, but it also ends the strong basis of the country's development. There are many jobs for the youth in their own country as well. Just work hard and move towards your destination. If the youth are not given a suitable job, then there will be a huge national wastage of human resources. They should be made partners in some positive work. If the activity of this manpower is used in the development projects of the country, then it can do wonders. Whenever the youth of the country were called upon to face any challenge, they did not lag behind. In times of natural calamities, youth come forward and contribute, be it earthquake or flood. The youth always worked day and night in helping the victims. All these factors affect and help in the development and specifically, youths can impact always the great towards society and social reformation. Swami Vivekananda, while talking upon the youth, had said a mantra of Kathopanishad- 'Uttishtt awake attainable varanibodhat.' That is, get up, awake, and don't stop till you reach your goal. There is no doubt that youth is an important part of the development of the country and society. Youth should provide their active contribution for the development of the country with Social, Youth and Nature Reformation. It is very important to involve youth in the work of improving society and nation-building and it should be done at the earliest and on a comprehensive level. This can only be possible with help of youngsters of this nation. With this, on one hand, you will be able to give their services to the country, on the other hand, it will also uplift yourself.

If we consider the needful aspects for social reformation then it makes me mention some of the major aspects if resolved can provide pace in national welfare. One of the major factors according to me is RURAL DEVELOPMENT, sitting in the metropolis, we create a different image of rural India, such as rural India with a quiet place, green fields, a peaceful life. But is it really at peace? Let's look at the aspects. Today rural India is in a state of crisis, isn't it? The reason for this is the increasing challenges in agriculture and also the lack of public interference. Net profit is not increasing at all due to the rising cost of farming, and not increasing the price of agricultural products in that proportion. It is even decreasing in some crops. For example, the gram was sold at Rs 6000–7000 per quintal last year, it is selling at Rs 3900–4500 per quintal this year and many variations can take place in the upcoming time. This is also the condition of potato farmers. The result of all this we can see in farmers' discontent, Dharna demonstration, suicides. There are many reasons for farmers to commit suicide. According to me the biggest reason for this is not getting the right and appropriate price for the produce. Another major reason is farmers' inability to repay their loans. In the villages, the farmers produce their own food. The problem arises when the farmers suddenly have to make some big expenditure like, girl's marriage or sudden health deteriorates or they want to do house construction. In this situation, the farmer has to take a loan. Which he is not in a position to repay due to his low income and he sometimes commits suicide out of boredom. This aspect of suicide also needs attention.

The second biggest problem is the growing distance between rural and urban India. After the liberalization of 1991, there has been a massive imbalance between rural and urban India. There are many reasons for this. Rural India could not take advantage of the job opportunities created after liberalization due to its decaying education system and urban India overtook it. For example, very few youths of rural India have employed in the IT sector, because they do not have enough skills due to poor education system, whereas urban youth took full advantage of the revolution in the IT sector and they went far ahead. Due to which naturally an inequality has arisen and it is increasing. Therefore, along with having 'equality of opportunities, it is also necessary that especially rural youth should be brought to the level of urban youth in the matter of education, only then they will be able to compete in the true sense and take advantage of the opportunities. Taking the issue of education forward, I would like to draw attention to the serious problem of copying in rural India. This problem is prevalent in a very dire form in my home district and its surrounding areas. This problem is like cancer and has taken the form of industry. People spend lakhs to get high school, intermediate, even bachelor-masters degree. And in the end, remain unemployed. Therefore, both the government and the society need to pay attention to the dissatisfaction and problems growing in rural India, then only a truly inclusive and happy India can be made.

An India where debt-ridden farmers will not need to commit suicide. If we consider then in major issues still lasting is Child labour on ground level. When young children are involved in economic activity for money, it is called child labor. The whole country is stuck in the roots of child labor, isn't it? It is one of the major social issues of India. Child labor affects the childhood of children. One of the reasons for child labor is the poverty of the country. To fill the stomach of the family, the lives of the children are sacrificed in the fire of child labor. Due to child labor, many times the children of the country are not able to get even basic education. Children also get money for wages. There are also many laws against child labor in our country, in which there is a provision of severe punishment. There are many reasons for child labor but some of the major reasons are illiteracy, poverty, and lack of awareness.

Due to poverty, children are sent to work in their childhood. There is a saying in India that the more hands you have, the more your stomach will be filled. Child labor is encouraged if someone in the house is very ill or the members earning the work are less. Due to poverty and due to financial constraints, children are not able to get a complete education. Child labor stops the mental and physical development of children. Due to this many diseases are born. Children are not able to get educated. As we know that youth is the future of the country but if the youth is not educated then how will the country progress? Children also die due to many diseases. Children who are victims of child labor are sometimes unable to lead a normal life. There are few friends in the life of such children and these children spend more time at work. This very major problem can be solved by making parents aware. What are the ill effects of child labor and the impact it will have on your child's life? This problem can also be solved by making children aware. If children are educated, the standard of living of the children will also improve and they will also get good jobs. The government needs to make stricter laws. People from poor families will have to be helped financially so that children can study.

CASTEISM is that narrow feeling of the members of the caste, which, ignoring the common interests of the nation and society, promotes the interests of the members of their caste and provides them opportunities to move forward. According to me, "The only religion is to follow Manavdharma (humanity) and the only caste is to be an Indian". Almost every society in the world, whether it is simply too simple or complex to complex, is more or less divided into some parts and some level is found in it. Earlier Indian society was divided into varnas i.e. earlier there was a varna system in India. The varna system was flexible, it was possible to move from one to the other. Gradually this movement decreased and with the conversion of varnas into castes it came to a complete halt. In ancient and medieval times, caste provided wide areas of interaction and social identity for its members. The caste was a society in itself within the larger society. Despite being in contact with other castes, a person lived a lot in his own caste, but he did not have blind devotion or blind allegiance to the caste. On the contrary, in the modern era, especially after independence, due to democratic politics, the individual began to understand caste as a means of promoting the interests of himself and his caste group, which strengthened the concept of casteism in the society. which ignores justice, justness, equality, and universal fraternity." "Racism is an unrelenting blind and supreme group devotion that ignores justice, justness, equality, and universal fraternity." Every member of a caste other members of the caste Because they have similar customs, similar religious ideas, common ancestors, or common occupation. All this also creates a feeling of loyalty to the caste. Due to the jajmani system, mutual relations were established between different castes. But with the end of this system, the mutual relations of different castes ended. This gave impetus to the ideas of casteism.

Due to the desire to raise the status of their caste, individuals try to advance the members of their caste in various fields, whether they have merit or not. Casteism has been born out of caste, so the word caste should not be used to end casteism. Just as through Article 18 of the Constitution, other titles other than military honors have been abolished, similarly, through the law, the addition of the word caste indicator to the name should be prohibited. Schools, colleges, Dharamsala, hostels, etc. The use of caste-specific words in naming should be legally prohibited. Ethnic organization, introduction conventions should be banned legally. Advertisements related to marriage on a caste basis should be banned. Casteism can also be stopped by encouraging inter-caste marriages. When people of one caste establish marriage relations with another caste, then casteism will automatically end. To stop casteism, the level of education should be raised so high that people should stay away from caste parochialism. Anti-caste public opinion through the media should be prepared. In rural society, caste is strictly followed.

Food-drinking, communion, travel, and friendship among different castes have been prevalent in the cities for a long time, but the caste-based distance and discrimination persists in the villages. In such a situation, urbanization should be developed at a rapid pace to weaken the caste system and make casteism ineffective. Educating people and spreading awareness can end this big problem. To bring change in society and eliminate casteism, the lesson of basic education is essential. Ending the process of superstition is also a solution. This practice may become extinct if everyone grows economically. Efforts should be made for this. Casteism should be boycotted through inter-caste conventions. We should live as one nation as united and we actually but we need some changes in the system and that is only possible by positive awareness.

POVERTY is the situation in which even the basic facilities of the people are not met, then it is called poverty. Basic facilities like no two meals a day, no house to stay, etc. Rural poverty is largely the result of low productivity and unemployment. The rural economy largely depends on agriculture. But agriculture in India is dependent on unpredictable monsoons, leading to uncertainty in yields. Lack of water, bad weather, and drought are also the main causes of poverty in rural areas. The government has tried to help such sections by making a poverty line card. Under this card, they will get a ration up to the specified limit in a month at a very cheap rate. Due to lack of education, they do not get good jobs and it increases poverty. The wheel of illiteracy and poverty runs together and creates poverty in society. Poverty is also caused due to casteism and the environment, like if there is a drought or if there is a flood, then agriculture is destroyed. There is no money for the destroyed crop and in this way poverty spreads. Where there will be more population and fewer opportunities, there will be poverty. The lower class has to depend on the rich people. They suffer from malnutrition because they do not get food at the right time. The physical development of poor people is also slow. Poverty can be relieved by giving more and more job opportunities. The government should focus on the economic development of the poor people. Children have to be given food along with education so that their bodies can also grow. Rural poverty is largely the result of low productivity and unemployment.

The rural economy largely depends on agriculture. But agriculture in India is dependent on unpredictable monsoons, leading to uncertainty in yields. Water scarcity, bad weather, and drought are also major causes of poverty in rural areas. Rural poverty is largely the result of low productivity and unemployment. The rural economy largely depends on agriculture. But agriculture in India is dependent on unpredictable monsoons, leading to uncertainty in yields. Water scarcity, bad weather, and drought are also major causes of poverty in rural areas. Poverty prevents people from accessing much-needed social means of well-being such as education and health needs. The direct consequences stemming from this problem are hunger, malnutrition, and susceptibility to diseases that have been identified as major problems around the world. It affects individuals in a socio-psychological way, as they are not able to afford simple recreational activities and become increasingly marginalized in society.

In CORRUPTION there are many problems in India, due to which the progress of the country is slow. Chief among them is unemployment, poverty, illiteracy, etc. But in all of them at present, if anyone is hindering the development of the country, then it is the problem of corruption. Today the whole country is worried about it. The work of hollowing out the roots of democracy is being done through this for a long time. And the extent of this problem is that for this even a former Prime Minister of India had to say that only twenty paise in rupees can reach the general public from Delhi. In fact, this situation has not been created in just one day. Just as India was about to get freedom from British slavery, it was about to get a chance to breathe in the open air, at the same time the ruling leaders divided the country and at the same time, it became clear that some elite sections were trying to satisfy their political hunger. For this, the country has become ready to keep the interest in jeopardy. Well, let it be passed. Leaving the matter of that time, if we look at the present situation, then a very frightening scene comes to the fore. Corruption has taken the entire nation in its lap. In fact, the entire system is responsible for corruption today. Even a common man is ready to hand over a closed envelope to the front person in order to get his work done in a government office quickly. Today 80 out of 100 men are trying to get this work done. And once someone starts getting such money illegally, then surely his craving will increase and the result of the same is being seen by the whole of India today. Yes, how can he be expected to conduct his office with honesty? The amount that he had invested for grooming his future, as soon as he gets a job in giving bribe, it is first equalized, then some are saved for grooming the future. It is sharp. Till this cycle is not broken, the common man will remain Abhimanyu in this Chakravyuh. The day the youth of the country starts getting both degree and job on the basis of his ability, then he will use this ability to remove corruption from the country. The war against corruption will be won when the common man opposes it and not when it accepts it. Avoid giving money to get our work done fast. If you saw someone doing a corruption complaint against that person.

Start change from your own self.

THE OVERPOPULATION. Today population has become a complex problem. Many problems arise due to its growth. The second part of this problem is the problem of unemployment, child marriage, want of a son, illiteracy, lack of information, social and religious beliefs, etc. All these reasons have to be completely destroyed. Possibly by these measures, the population growth will be stopped. This is the root of many problems like poverty, unemployment, environmental problem, corruption, etc. Due to this, there is the moral degradation of the citizens. As a result, the decline of the national character is natural. It also has an effect on the economy. Many efforts have been made by the government, extensive publicity work has been done regarding family planning through mass communication and is being done continuously. The population can also be called the power of the nation. The government can easily get the big works done by the people force in less time and less cost. The country can have an advanced army ready for the defense and peace system of the country. It is also beneficial due to more population. But due to more population growth than necessary, the profit is less and the loss is more. Today the problem of the population has taken the form of a very formidable problem. Many problems have arisen from this problem. Work is being done to solve this problem over the years. First of all 'Family Planning' was started in India in 1952.

The country's first woman Prime Minister had also taken concrete steps for 'family planning, but due to lack of correct information, she had to be a victim of criticism from most of the public. In those who were operated, they used to blame the operation itself for being unwell due to other reasons. No one understood the love behind his country. Due to ignorance, some people protested because there was a lack of awareness. "Hand burning while doing home" has been said to happen with Indiraji, the government has always been trying to solve this problem. Family planning has been widely disseminated through mass media and is continuously engaged. Many voluntary organizations are working to solve this problem. The age of marriage has been fixed by the government, child marriage has been banned, provision of punishment has also been made. In a family which has only one daughter, many facilities have been given for that daughter. Unless every citizen of the country cooperates in this problem, it is difficult to solve this problem. Along with the government, every human will have to be aware. If everyone pays attention together, then the problem of environment, the problem of unemployment, the problems of the place will be solved.

Hence the need for awareness.

ILLITERACY means not being able to write and read. This problem is due to the high population and poverty in India. Illiteracy is one of the reasons for the weakness of the country's economic system. If the youth of the country gets educated, then no one can stop that country from becoming a progressive country. If parents are not educated, then they are unable to tell the importance of education to their children. Due to child labor, children do not get full opportunities, this is also one of the reasons for going to school. Poverty is also an important cause of illiteracy. Due to high fees in schools, parents are unable to send their children to school. Poverty increases and there is a decline in the standard of living of the family. Can't get good jobs. Due to not being educated, crimes increase and the coming generation also remains illiterate. Illiteracy can be eradicated through education. The government should encourage poor children to be educated in schools. Children and their parents will have to be made aware of books by going to the slums. Poor children will have to be provided education near their homes.

A large percentage of children are deprived of even basic primary school education due to major social problems like caste discrimination, child marriage, child labour. Illiteracy in India is accentuated by the huge gender bias that exists against females in terms of education. A girl child is denied an education by stating illogical reasons like her existence is only to take care of her family and kids. The government alone cannot solve the vast problem of illiteracy in the country. It is not possible to achieve the objective of total eradication of illiteracy entirely through governmental efforts. The government can undoubtedly take cognizance of the situation, can identify the agencies, institutions, and individuals can act as a catalytic agent to provide human material and financial resources, but the government cannot promote literacy all by itself. The provision of free education in schools, colleges, and universities by the government can play a major role in reducing the level of illiteracy in a country by getting more people to school. Since some people fail to attend school due to a lack of money to pay for the fees, offering free education can increase the number of people attending school and subsequently reduce illiteracy levels within a society. Creating awareness about the importance of education can help people understand why they need to go to school.

Non-governmental organizations, government agencies, and other concerned parties should put in place deliberate measures to create awareness in society and reduce the number of people who are unable to read and write.

GENDER INEQUALITY is the foundation of a beautiful and secure society on which the building of development can be built. What is gender equality? After all, why has it become an essential element for any society and nation? Is it relevant in a changing society? Gender equality does not mean that every person in the society should belong to one gender, but gender equality simply means equal rights, responsibilities, and employment opportunities of women and men in the society. Because of this fact, 17 Sustainable Development Goals were placed under Agenda 2030 at the high-level meeting of the United Nations General Assembly in September 2015, which was accepted by 193 countries including India. These goals also include the topic of gender equality under Sustainable Development Goal 5. It is clear that gender equality is very important for the development of our society. Women and men are the basic pillars of society. Gender inequality in society is a deliberately created gap, which makes the journey to achieve the level of equality very difficult. Talking about the different areas of gender inequality, along with the social, economic, and political fields, the scientific field, the entertainment sector, the medical field, and the sports sector are prominent. National Science Day was organized on 28 February with the theme 'Women in Science'. This is a great attempt to underline the role of women in the field of science, but we still have miles to go to bridge this gap of gender inequality. In this article, not only will the reasons for gender inequality be discussed but an attempt will be made to find a solution to this problem. There is a gradual change in the mindset of society as a result of which issues related to women are being discussed seriously. . Due to the activeness of the government and courts on issues like triple talaq, entry to Haji Ali Dargah, women are being given their rights. India is continuously making good efforts in the field of political participation, as a result of which India has been ranked 18th among other points on the Global Gender Gap Index-2020 on Political Empowerment and Participation Standards. The participation of women in the cabinet has already increased to 23% and in this India is ranked 69th in the world. India took further actions to implement Mexico

Action Plan (1975), the Nairobi Provident Strategies

(1985) and the "Beijing Declaration and Platform for

Action for the 21st Century" adopted by the United Nations General Assembly Session on Gender Equality and Development and Peace and Initiatives" on global initiatives for gender equality. Efforts are being made for women empowerment through schemes like 'Beti Bachao Beti Padhao', 'One Stop Center Scheme', 'Women Helpline Scheme', and 'Mahila Shakti Kendra'. As a result of the implementation of these schemes, progress is being seen in the sex ratio and educational enrollment of girls. Mudra and other women-centric schemes are being run for self-reliance in the economic field.

OLD AGE HOMES Reverence for one's parents is deeply bedded in Indian families. Children suppose it their moral duty to look after their aged parents and elders. In the last many decades, our society has experienced a massive metamorphosis in terms of family structure. As a consequence of the social Metamorphosis and evolving cultures, numerous of the aged parents are landing in old age homes. The accumulating of nuclear families especially in civic India has led to a steadily adding number of old age homes. The increase in old age homes in the metropolitan metropolises isn't a good development. Over three decades ago, the study of aged parents being transferred to the old age homes wasn't fluently accepted in our country due to traditional mindset and artistic morality," says Bangaloregrounded Kishore Joseph, trustee, Omasharm Trust Old Age Care which presently serves an aggregate of 65 resident elders. The most egregious reason for this trend is the migration of children from their motherlands to metropolitan metropolises in hunt of better education, jobs, and bettered cultures. While the youngish generation has no difficulty in moving out of their maternal homes and conforming to new cultures, the senior population chooses to remain back due to the attached sentiments of the place. Also, numerous children can not take care of their aged parents with habitual health issues. Some elders find it delicate to manage with their sons-in-law and grandchildren, due to differences in values and mindset. " Utmost of the aged parents who are brought into the homes are over 65 Times old and are bedridden. We take care of these seniors like our own parents. The children do visit them at least formerly a month or for the birthdays and anniversaries," affirms Joseph. In the original stages, any senior parent who comes to the old age home is veritably reticent to live then. Further, it isn't easy for them to get acclimated to a different air at their age. Ultimately, they acclimate to the new terrain and also develop lasting bonds with other resides. They sluggishly tend to accept the old age homes as their own home," says Chennai- grounded Kunjamma Thomas, trustee of Maria's old age home that caters to over 60 resident elders. Further, though old age homes are mushrooming in the metropolises, not all old age homes can go to give quality service and care. Utmost of them are operated in rented demesne and are not suitable to meet their yearly recreating charges which are veritably high. Middle-class families can not go through these charges. " The aged parents we've hail from middle-class families. These families find the charges too extravagant. Numerous times, children don't show up after three or four months. We also take the responsibility on our shoulders of bearing their charges, through donations. It should be the appanage of the government to make sanctum homes for the elderly citizens and also take care of them," delineates Joseph. There's also a positive side to this heart-breaking story. Numerous working children are trying hard to look after their parents in their own homes. They're hiring nurses to take care of their aged parents in the metropolises while they're at work. Some others have made security arrangements for the senior, like installing CCTV cameras to watch over them while they're at work. In some cases, when the children themselves turn old and can not take care of their own aged parents, only also they're put into old age homes. " It's touching to see some children and grandchildren making all possible sweats to take care of their own parents in their own homes. The senior love care and attention which they earn from their loved bones and in their own homes, " concludes Thomas. The joint family system in India has been providing social, economic, and mental security to the elderly. Therefore, efforts should be made to prevent its disintegration. Community life in traditional Indian society did not allow the elderly to realize any of their problems. Therefore, measures should be taken to reinvigorate such community life. Means of healthy entertainment should be provided for the elderly. To solve the problem of old age, it is also very important that we should accept old age as an inevitability of life. , not as a burden. Free arrangements should be made for the health problems of the elderly. Also, the health insurance system should be started for senior citizens at a very low premium. The amount of old-age pension scheme should be increased. A family environment should be arranged for the elderly. The Central Social Welfare Board has planned to organize old houses and cradle houses in one place so that the elderly people can enjoy the activities of the children and they can enjoy the full enjoyment of life.

Due to limitations of space and time in this book we are going to publish our second edition, which will cover the detailed perspective with all root level problems and solutions. This book contains a novel highlighting approach for you, do think about it and you will for sure improve your knowledge with a wide-angle intellectual mindset. Reader you have this book in your hand which means you have the potential and desire to pace our national development. Wake up, start with yourself. The future of the nation depends on you.

SECTION-3

EMPOWERING NATURE REFORMATION

From Sustainable to Sustainability of Development can be Nature Reformation. In the present era, the biggest problem of environmental imbalance is global warming and due to which the temperature of the earth is increasing and the steps of human life are moving towards destruction. It is really a challenge for all of us, as youngsters of this nation you can play a vital role in conservation and reformation. At such a time, if we do not take any big step to save the environment, then the day is not far when our very existence will be in danger. The future of the Earth and its inhabitants depend on environmental maintenance and preservation related to our capabilities. In this context, the concept of sustainable development has been developed for the sustainable use and enhancement of the environment. Sustainability is an inherent characteristic of all-natural environmental systems, which accepts human intervention to a minimum level. It relates to the ability of a system to maintain and maintain its continuous flow, as a result of which that system is able to maintain its healthy existence. Due to human use of environmental resources and interference in environmental systems, this built-in capacity gets distorted, making it unsustainable. So I feel the need to talk to conserve and save nature by reforming it with proper perspective in this chapter. If we consider it, on the contrary, economists argue that exploitation and degradation of resources encourage research and development and lead to the discovery of new alternatives to resources, but every possibility also has a limit. Conservationists and ecologists were aware of the sustainability of natural environmental systems for a long time, but the concept of convergent development was developed only two decades ago.

"Composite development is to meet the needs of the present generation without reducing the ability of the future generation to meet their own needs." The following concepts are included in the concept of sustainable development: The concept of needs should be considered with special emphasis on the needs of the poor people of the world. The environmental capacity to meet current and future needs should be considered within the limits set by technology and social organization. It has long been recognized that the future of the Earth and its inhabitants are based on our ability to preserve and conserve nature. The environment becomes unbalanced as soon as there is a decrease in our abilities to save the nature-given subsistence system. In this context, the following topics related to sustainable development are important to make each and everyone aware: Full utilization of all renewable resources is unionized. The diversity of life on earth is preserved. The degradation of natural environmental systems has been reduced. Taking care of the environment is the responsibility of every person. But today, due to neglecting this responsibility towards the environment, pollution is spreading. While fulfilling our needs, we did not know when we had ruined the nature-environment so much. Not only this, we have also suffered the brunt of it. Somewhere cities are drying up and somewhere there is a disaster-like flood. Somewhere there is a mountain of garbage and somewhere there is destruction due to earthquake. Despite all this, we have not stopped exploiting nature. You may have tried to save electricity or water at your own level many times but you have thought that what will happen if you do this alone? To overcome this problem, the whole world needs to be united. Let us know today, those small special measures, by starting from home itself, you can get control over this problem in this chapter. Measures to control pollution can be-To prevent wastage of water, first of all, try that no tap is dripping in the house. In such a situation, get the leaking taps repaired as soon as possible. Apart from this, if you ever see any uncontrolled or poorly flowing government pipeline, do not ignore it. Report it to the concerned department immediately. Another way to save the environment is that instead of filling water in the bathtub, fill the bucket with water and take a bath with a mug. Doing this will save water. While using the printer, keep in mind that the paper used in it should be used from both sides. Apart from this, keep some space in the courtyard of your house for trees and plants. Along with giving greenery, they also keep the temperature low. To save the environment, plant more and more trees and plants. Apart from this, if you eat any fruit during the journey, then stop for a while and bury its kernels in the soil. Be it your birthday or children's birthday or any memorable moment, make those memories permanent by planting trees. Always use reusable bags to buy goods from the market, to give gifts or to bring vegetables, etc. Smoking is not only injurious to health but it also pollutes the air. By not smoking, the environment can be saved by reducing air pollution. Today the biggest reason for pollution is also the number of increasing vehicles. In such a situation, to prevent air pollution, take proper care of your vehicles and keep checking pollution from time to time. By doing this you can contribute towards environmental protection and conservation.

The environment is related to those living and non-living things, which are present around us, and whose existence is very important for us. It includes air, water, soil, humans, animals, and birds, etc. Although living in a city, town, or village, we see that the environment and place around us was actually a natural place such as a desert, forest, or even a river, etc. have been transformed into roads or factories. Our entire surroundings and fauna, including air, water, and sunlight, etc. Apart from this, living organisms such as animals, birds, trees, plants, etc., contribute to development and growth. Human beings together create the environment. The environment of today's industrial and urban areas includes paved roads, multi-story concrete buildings, and skyscrapers. Their main objective is to create facilities for the growing population and to make the life of the rich and elite class comfortable and luxurious. However, despite this industrial and urban movement, man's dependence on natural resources remains the same as before. Air is used by us for respiration, water is used for drinking and other daily activities, not only this, the food we eat is also many types of plants, animals, birds and vegetables, milk. Obtained from eggs etc. Keeping these needs in mind, the protection of these resources has become very important. The most important thing at this time is that we have to stop the misuse of these resources and use them very judiciously because their rapid use by the earth cannot be tolerated anymore. The achievement of this goal is possible only through sustainable development. Apart from this, there is also a need to control the liquid and solid by-products that are dumped in the form of waste by the industrial units, as they increase pollution. Due to which many diseases related to cancer and stomach and intestine arise. This is possible only when we leave the dependence on the government and personally take necessary steps to solve this problem. The imbalance of nature and the deteriorating environment is an important problem for the whole world today. As a result of the deteriorating climate, we are seeing such incidents which are creating a dreadful scene for mankind. Despite this we are only worrying for years, The percentage of effort that should be made on the ground is very less. We want to earn money and wealth for the coming generation, but we do not want to leave a pleasant environment and living environment for them.

I think Forests also play a large role in maintaining the water cycle, providing habitat for animals, maintaining the environmental balance, and soil erosion. Without forests, it is not possible to rain or breathe pure air for us but due to the explosive growth rate of the human population, the need for more land for survival and for agricultural purposes is increasing. That is why deforestation is being done continuously for wood, fuel, agriculture, home, and other purposes. People are converting forests into cities to make them a place to live. Forests are very important for the survival of humanity but by not taking steps to rejuvenate them and plant new trees, humans are destroying the existing forests. Instead of planting trees, deforestation is happening at a faster rate, that is, the plantation is not happening at the rate at which forests are being cut. If deforestation continues like this, the situation will worsen during the summer season. Apart from the increase in floods, landslides, and storms, etc., the weather will remain dry throughout the year. Due to the negative changes in the environment, deforestation is already affecting human life in a big way. Thus our tiny home Earth is rapidly heading towards the consequences of an unprecedented crisis. Paper is made from the pulp of trees. This has already attracted the attention of environmentalists even before the increasing consumption of paper and the reduction of trees for manufacturing paper around the world. Trees are being cut for many years for the purpose of development work. Increasing urban population is one of the major causes of deforestation.

Forests are being cleared for large scale construction of roads, mineral exploitation, and industrial expansion, to meet residential and industrial needs such as large-scale housing development. Expansion of roads is also a major reason for illegal felling of trees where people cut down trees by taking advantage of doubt without obtaining permission of the authorities. Forests are very essential for the survival of life on earth. They play an important role in maintaining the water cycle by making it rain. Yet their existence is under threat due to increasing human greed. The issue of deforestation has emerged as a major environmental and social problem that has assumed a monstrous shape. Due to deforestation, ecological and environmental imbalances arise due to which problems have arisen in human life. The increasing rate of deforestation is itself a warning to save the existence of life on earth. Conservation of forests is important for reducing the amount of carbon dioxide in the environment as well as for a fresh and healthy supply of oxygen. India's environmental problems include various natural hazards, notably cyclones and annual monsoon floods, population growth, increasing individual consumption, industrialization, infrastructural development, poor agricultural practices, and unequal distribution of resources, and have led to excessive human exposure to India's natural environment.

Climate change Patterns of average weather conditions, do you know about this? This change in climate conditions can be natural as well as the result of human activities. The greenhouse effect and global warming are believed to be the result of human actions, which after the Industrial Revolution caused carbon dioxide released by humans from industries. It is the result of the increase in the amount of gas in the atmosphere. Scientists have been constantly warning about the dangers of climate change. The greenhouse effect or greenhouse effect is a natural process by which certain gases present in the atmosphere of a planet or satellite help to make the temperature of the atmosphere relatively higher. These greenhouse gases include carbon dioxide, water vapor, methane, etc. Mainly, the balance between the energy received from the sun and its loss determines the climate and temperature balance of our earth. This energy is distributed around the world by winds, ocean currents, and other systems and affects the climate of different regions.

Since the beginning of time, the environment has helped us establish relationships with flora and fauna, which has ensured our life. Nature has given us many gifts such as water, sunlight, air, animals and fossil fuels, etc., through which these things have made our planet habitable. Due to the fireworks of Diwali, the climate of all the cities of the country including Delhi, Mumbai has become poisonous. After the end of Diwali, the problems related to it come to the fore. Like every year, due to air pollution and noise pollution, people are upset this year too. Diwali crackers bring smoke and noise along with the light. It is said that in the last five years, the demand for firecrackers has increased 10 times. This time the record of air pollution was broken and there was a lot of poison in the air due to fireworks. As always, it had the biggest impact on patients, children, and the elderly. Doctors say that every year after Diwali in the same way, people's health is affected. If sick, even healthy people are falling ill due to pollution. The environment here is also becoming poisonous due to deforestation, increasing vehicles, and fireworks around in the environment. What to talk about the country's capital, Delhi is considered to be the most polluted city in the country after Diwali. On the second number, the names of cities like Faridabad then Lucknow, Kanpur, Patna, Mumbai, and Agra can be taken. Today, from tomorrow morning, a sheet of harmful smog starts appearing in Delhi NCR. Scientists believe that the situation was worse due to worsening weather conditions compared to the last time. On the other hand, the data of the

Pollution Control Board shows that now the air pollution index of Delhi reaches a very dangerous level. Recently, Delhi became the most polluted city in the country with a pollution index of 450 estimates. Actually, crackers are made from a mixture of many toxic elements including sulfur. The sulfur content is the highest in these, so the more firecrackers are fired, the more the level of sulfur dioxide in the air increases. Despite this, people burst firecrackers fiercely on new year and many more programs like birthdays, the effect of which is now coming to the fore. According to the World Health Organization, every year in India, about 6 lakh people suffer untimely cheeks due to pollution-related reasons. However, very few people in India are aware of its horrors. Therefore, with the aim of making people aware, the Modi government at the Centre has recently given priority to it and has started telling them how is the air quality of the area where they live. With this, people can become aware of this themselves and can play their role in preventing the spread of pollution. On this, it has been told in a media report that at present, about 247 cities of the country have some degree of air quality monitoring mechanism, so that the surroundings It is easy to know about the daily air quality. However, all this is surprising for us. Because we thought that after all the efforts, the awareness has increased and the youth are also loving the environment and destroying the environment. Lakhs of appeals were made not to burn firecrackers. Even after that, the record of the last year was broken. Actually, the environment will not be safe from anyone's understanding. For this everyone has to cooperate. According to experts, while firecrackers emit poisonous gases like sulfur dioxide, carbon dioxide, monodioxide, which harm the life on earth. The reason is clear that the reason for life is Life is necessary for life and the sequence of breaths in life is a continuous process. Therefore, when the poison is dissolved in the air, then you cannot escape from this poison. Doctors say that the air mixed with sulfur nitrous as well as fine particles of iron When you breathe in, these toxic particles remain in the lungs, which makes your lungs very weak.

"No generation has a monopoly on this earth, we are all here to live - the price of which we also have to pay" Margaret Thatcher's statement reflects our temporary relationship with nature. In spite of all the gifts provided by the earth to make our life easier and make this planet habitable, such as air, sunlight, water, animals, and minerals, etc. They are not deterred from exploiting the resources. To save our mother earth (life on earth), we need to save the existing god in our environment. To meet the current needs of our increasing population level, we are consuming our natural resources indiscriminately without thinking. We are not worrying about our future generation also. In this way, the biggest concern in today's time is that we need to take strict steps to protect our renewable and non-renewable resources and to protect our earth. Environmental protection is not only the work of the government, for this, our own contribution as a person is also very important. Knowingly or unknowingly, we contribute to pollution every day. Therefore, it is our duty as a consumer to make use of the gifts of nature, to promote water conservation and participate in the reuse and recycling of goods, stop wastage of resources like electricity and water, etc. By all these small measures, we can bring about a very effective change in the condition of our planet. On turning the pages of history, it is known that our ancestors were more concerned about environmental protection than us. For this, we can see Sunderlal Bahuguna as an example, who started the Chipko movement for the protection of forest resources. Similarly, Medha Patekar had made effective efforts for environmental protection for the tribal people, who were negatively affected by the dam being built on the Narmada river. In today's time as a youth, it is our responsibility to make similar efforts for environmental protection. By taking some small measures, we can give our cooperation in saving nature: We should promote the concept of 3R, under which tasks like reduce, recycle, reuse are included. In which we can take measures like reducing the excessive use of non-renewable energy sources, such as using iron waste to make iron. Use of energy-saving products like tube lights and bulbs. Use less paper and wood Use ebooks and e-papers as much as possible.

Minimizing the use of fossil fuels using measures such as walking, carpools, or public transportation to get around and Eco-friendly products. Use jute or cloth bags instead of plastic bags. Using reusable batteries and solar panels. Reducing the use of chemical fertilizers and setting up compost bins for making manure from cow dung and other biomass organically. By the way, many laws and schemes have also been established by the government for the protection of nature and wildlife. But is it not our personal responsibility? It is our duty personally that every person should contribute our contribution in environmental protection and secure the future of our coming generations because at present it is being used the most by us. This can be understood very simply in the words of Lester Brown, "We have not received this earth from our ancestors, but we have taken it from our future generations".

"She reminds our generations:
To make ourselves luxurious,
Crossed all limits to harm glorious.
To care the inheritance of ancient,
We forget the liability to secure present.
Aren't we greedy about ourselves?
For we have destroyed the nature herself.
She's the mother, a voracious divine,
Making her regret, the deeds lifetime.

Instead being a perfect inherent,
Disrespected the nature, our parent.
Her anger booms in calamities,
We witness the opposite divinities.
The floods, tsunami and droughts,
Yeah! It's the cursed deeds caused.
We pray the almighty for recovery,
And bow them, felt, being guilty.
Can't we do before the consequence?
The ego doesn't let this happens.
This is what breaks the arrogance.
Because, Sheds the mother of incarnations,
The divine of all manifestations.
Making the youth reminds their Generations!!!"

Due to limitations of space and time in this book we have tried to create awareness and highlight major points. We are going to publish our second edition, which will cover the detailed perspective with all root level problems and solutions. This book contains a novel highlighting approach for you readers, do think about it and you will for sure improve your knowledge with a wide-angle intellectual mindset. Friends you have this book in your hand that means you have the potential and desire to pace our national development. Wake up, start with yourself.

The future of the nation depends on you.

About The Author

KETAN VILAS FIRKE (AUTHOR)

Ketan V. Firke is a young student, socialist personality, and Indian writer belonging to the Jalgaon district in the state of Maharashtra. The author is an aspiring Engineer and "The Empowering Uniqueness – Towards social Youth and Nature Reformation" book is written by the author at the age of 18. The author is the founder of the Eco-Indium Welfare activity in Maharashtra-India. The author is interested in reading more and more books and experimenting with concepts for the betterment of society and humankind.

The author is working peacefully and democratically across Maharashtra in the social and environmental movement of India with the power of youth. Youths from Khandesh (Jalgaon) and Maharashtra know and proudly appreciate the author as Krushimitra, Speaker, Writer, and Activist.

The author specifically follows a formula of "Only one religion is humanism, only one caste is Indian".

As a speaker, the author has worked at length on issues on the ground and by taking seminars, lectures, and workshops for free on various subjects pertaining to mental peace, human life, stress relief, and modern psychology for which he holds great appreciation by youths.

The activity started by the author, "Eco Indium welfare activity" is specifically working on Environment, climate change, agricultural and rural development with Social, Youth and Nature Reformation. This is an activity by the youths for the youths towards National welfare. Free of cost mental peace and meditation workshops, guiding seminars for farmers, free food for roaders, a free medical check-up for tribal, Gramsanjeevini program, Apangkranti, No more Vrudhashrams, Encouragement training, Establishing organized and organic food security, Go Green with tree walk and many more programs are arranged by author with a team of youths.

The Word INDIUM means In National Development of Indian Universal Moment and it is the oath followed by every member. Eco- Indium activity specifies the author's work and experience.

You can reach the author on ketanfirke1112@gmail.com

About The Co-author

Pushpak T. Chaudhari

Pushpak Tushar Chaudhari is a young student , socialist personality & Indian writer belonging to the Jalgaon district is the state of Maharashtra. The co- author is an aspiring engineer and "The Empowering Uniqueness- Towards Social Youth and Nature Reformation" book have a lot of contribution by the co-author. The co-author is the co-founder of The Trustworthiness Foundation & working member of Eco-Indium Welfare activity in Maharashtra,India. The Co-author is interested in reading lots of books and write on many topics related to Youth & Nature.

The co-author is working with his team across Maharashtra in youth & social activities of India with power of youth. People from proudly appreciate the co-author as Yuva , Pasumitra & writer.

The co-author specifically follow, "Unity to be real must stand the severest strain without breaking".

As a social worker, the co-author has worked with his team

during the time of covid 19 by creating awareness among people to ware mask, washing hands and take care of their health followed bay doing volunteering at covid vaccination centre in different cities of Jalgaon district, Maharashtra

The activity started by the co-author "Trustworthiness" is specifically working on helping poor and needy people, Environment and rural development. This activity provide free of cost food to needy and tribal people and arranging guiding seminar of rural development along with free medical campaign for tribal & rural people.

The co-author also like to collect coins, notes and stamps. The co-author is also good at sports like running and cricket.

You can reach to co-author at:- pushchaudhari6@gmail.com

www.ingramcontent.com/pod-product-compliance
Lightning Source LLC
Chambersburg PA
CBHW060539160726
47991CB00001B/388